First Penthouse Dwellers of America

by
Ruth M. Underhill
with photographs by
Lilian J. Reichard

William Gannon · Santa Fe · 1976

This edition, published in 1976 by William Gannon, is a reprint of the edition published by J. J. Augustin in 1938.

clothbound edition ISBN 0-88307-525-3

paperbound edition ISBN 0-88307-526-1

Library of Congress Catalog Card Number 75-23849

Address all orders and inquiries to:

William Gannon, publisher
P.O. Box 2610
Santa Fe, New Mexico 87501

TABLE OF CONTENTS

Foreword: Indian Americans of the
            Pueblos ~ Who are they?   v

List of Photographs   ix

Chapter 1: The first Immigrants   1

Chapter 2: The Peaceful Hopi   25

Chapter 3: Zuni the Center   57

Chapter 4: The Warriors of Keres   85

Chapter 5: The Catholic Tewa   109

Chapter 6: Taos by the Buffalo Country   131

iii

FOREWORD

Indian Americans of the Pueblos
Who are they?

Through the streets of cities in the American Southwest, walk certain *brilliantly colored figures*, swathed in blankets and *with bright headbands over* long black *hair cut across the forehead like that of a medieval page.* They pass quietly through the modern throng, bearing bundles of rugs on their backs or dangling strings of silver and turquoise. Or they sit beneath a roadside shelter of boughs, the pottery of their ancient craft before the days of the potter's wheel, spread out before them.

These are the Pueblo Indians. Those of their fellow Americans whose idea of an Indian is summed up in an eagle feather, a tomahawk and a blood curdling whoop wonder where to place them in the history of our country. They are even more puzzled to learn that Pueblo is not the name of a tribe. It is merely the Spanish word for village and is applied to people who speak four different languages, pointing to at least four different places of origin. The peaceful Hopi, on the remote mesas of Arizona; the gentle Zuni, silversmiths and artists in

v

pageantry; the Keres, with their traditions of war and mighty magic; the Tanoans, with their beautiful blend of Catholic and pagan ceremony. All of these are so different that in time they can be distinguished on sight, not only by the build, the face, the costume, the craft work which, perhaps, they have for sale, but by the temperament and the very manner.

The Pueblos were little city-states in the olden days and they have remained so. They are farming people who, through centuries of labor and discovery, have worked out for themselves a method of livelihood, a government, and a religion. When hunting and fighting became things of the past in America, these villagers did not have to seek desperately for a new life. In their hidden valleys and on their distant mesas, they continued to till their fields, to rule their towns and to usher the year on its course with complicated ceremonies.

Meanwhile, white men have been filling up the country first with Spaniards, then with other Whites. In the course of that history, there have been passionate efforts to change the Pueblo Indians; there has been oppression, there has been neglect, there has been fumbling kindness. Through most of that time, the opinion of the white man has been that these were belated wanderers, off the right track of civilization who would be grateful for being shown the first steps to it. Bitter disappointments and better thinking have somewhat changed that point of view. To the white man human progress now looks not so much like a straight line with himself as its culmination, as like a series of feelers, meandering in all directions like runlets from a pool. One of these runlets—or several of them—has reached the Southwest.

vi

The white man looks up from his absorption to see here a life peaceful, religious, stable, yet different from his own. How, he begins to inquire, do these fellow citizens live? Have they the same emotions as himself? What interests them? Above all, what is their relationship to the white neighbors around them? What form of cooperation will be found for all in their common country?

RUTH M. UNDERHILL

Photographs

I

....brilliantly colored figures .... with bright headbands over .... hair cut across the forehead like that of a mediæval page. (p. 4)

The answer is corn. (p. 5)

And then perhaps a bone, or even a whole skeleton. (p. 12)

....the straight black hair, high cheekbones, slanting eyes .... called Mongolian. (p. 12)

These house ruins are now some rods from a wound in the earth called an arroyo.... (p. 12)

We may think of the bare mesa behind the pueblo .... as having been as well wooded as some of the mountain tops today. (p. 13)

....the woman....plastered the house as does her descendant today.... (p. 20)

In the court in front were sunk the great windowless rooms which the Spaniards called estufas or stoves. (p. 20)

....the great apartment houses ....can still be seen, almost completely unearthed. (p. 20)

Others with their well-preserved masonry, oddly-shaped doorways, curved kiva walls, holes through which beams once protruded and, in cases, even the beams themselves.... (p. 21)

....where the apartment houses went up in shelf-like caves.... (p. 28)

....with their blank rear walls for defense and with lookout towers.... (p. 28)

The Spaniards had learned from the Moors to use a chimney, and the observant pueblo people copied it, using a pile of bottomless pots (San Ildefonso). (p. 28)

Must there be school? Yes, the pueblos want it. (p. 28)

2

....pushing your car around rocky corners edged with sky.... (p. 36)

....to gaze out over the cloud-shadowed desert.... (p. 37)

....at the base of the mesa you may note a spring with a sprig of evergreen planted by its brink.... (p. 44)

....and naked children find their one real bathtub.... (p. 44)

....now he may have clothes from the mail order house.... (p. 44)

....when Hopi children play.... (p. 45)

It takes hours to grind first on the coarse slab.... (p. 52)

If she lives on First Mesa she will make pottery.... (p. 53)

The hardest part of the tray is to get it started.... (p. 60)

The mother will have a bee at which many of her friends make centers. (p. 60)

When you buy one of these products of Hopi craft, a waste basket for example, you will know it comes from Third Mesa. (p. 60)

....rule of women? Not in the least. Just a convenient way of counting descent. (p.61)

....they meet in the kiva.... (p. 68)

The Hopi men make dolls to represent these kachinas.... (p. 68)

3

The fields by the river glow a brilliant green.... (p. 68)

....drive through modern streets among houses.... no longer terraced. (p. 69)

Through a window a man....may be seen bending over the delicate jewelry.... (p. 76)

Others carry water jars on their heads as of old.... (p. 76)

Near the houses are the...."waffle-gardens".... (p. 76)

....drive....horses round and round....till their hoofs have pounded out the grains. (p. 77)

If she makes pots now she makes them for sale. (p. 84)

Somehow the art of sewing beads....got started.... (p. 84)

....the Navajo man is long-limbed and relaxed, the Comanche has a war bonnet.... (p. 84)

Lily who is less than two years old attempts to sew beads along with her mother and her aunts. (p. 85)

Meantime he sees the masked gods dance in the plaza.... (p. 92)

X

4

.... winding dusty paths above which the terraced houses .... are piled. (p. 92)

Long ladders lead to the upper storeys. (p. 92)

.... until suddenly we come upon a party repairing a house. (p. 93)

The villagers point to the cliff called by the Whites the Enchanted Mesa. (p. 100)

Acoma's church is still standing.... (p. 101)

.... and below it are corrals.... (p. 108)

.... in which burros are kept.... (p. 108)

.... the women, children .... sit under shelters.... (p. 108)

5

Catholic .... they were in much sincerity.... (p. 109)

.... they had kept their ancient ceremonies.... (p. 116)

.... the whole town .... may turn out in its ancient dress.... (p. 117)

.... a day on which the whole village is open.... (p. 124)

.... to guests of all kinds. (p. 124)

If it is the modern San Ildefonso you see.... shops of pottery makers. (p. 124)

Maria Martinez of San Ildefonso used to bring her pots to Santa Fe.... (p. 125)

6

Just beneath the mountain wall.... perches Taos. (p. 132)

Each has its own kivas.... (p. 133)

.... mother and child.... (p. 140)

She follows her mother to the great hive-shaped oven which stands outside the house.... (p. 140)

.... clothespins swinging against a puffy sky beside oldtime ladders over new window frames with glass. (p. 140)

xi

Pueblo is a name used to designate all the Indians who live in towns (Spanish, pueblo, town) in the Southwest.

There are many of them; the following are the best known. They are placed in the order in which they are pictured in this book; those especially described *in italics*. The main headings are made on the basis of language, sub-headings within a language family:

At the west:
 Hopi
 Zuni
Near the center:
 Keres:
  San Felipe
  Cochiti
  Santo Domingo
  Santa Ana
  Acoma
  Laguna

At the east:
 Tanoan, Tewa:
  San Juan
  Santa Clara
  San Ildefonso
  Nambe
  Tesuque
  Pojoaque
  Jemez
  Pecos (extinct)
 Tanoan , Tiwa (Tigua):
  Taos
  Picuris
  Sandia
  Isleta

1

The first Immigrants

The high, bare country where the Pueblos stand stretches like a three-cornered shelf across the upper part of Arizona and New Mexico. It represents the spreading end of the Rockies and from it there is a drop of four thousand feet to the desert country below. Down there, among the cactus and the shimmering lizards, lies another land with another history. But he who follows the history of the Pueblos prowls through the canyons of the waterless plateau with its brilliant sky, wild thunderstorms, glaring heat and windy chill.

In places the plains are barren and gashed as an excavation, their only color the earthen mixture of iron, red as burnt orange, yellow clay, crumbled black lava. Then, on a sudden rise, there are patches of juniper, its green almost smothered in hyacinth-blue berries and of pinyon, the little twisted pine trees, which bear delicious nuts and

I

whose roots oozing tar, burn in the campfire with a gorgeous red flame and black smoke. It is not a country for deer and duck and fish, the standby of the hunting Indian. Rabbits furnish the only meat and the wild vegetables are pinyon nuts with a few seeds and herbs. Yet in all the land now covered by the United States, here it was that one of the most complicated civilizations grew up.

The answer is corn. People could live on that plateau only if they were farmers and had their food growing beside them. Food is the answer to most of the wanderings and the habits of early people at grips with nature. Where they have plenty of food, they can settle down and build houses. Many families can live together, instead of separating, each to its own hunting field. Where many live together they can institute a government. They can plan ceremonies for all the year, knowing that all will be present to take part. So a whole civilization grew up on that tail of the Rockies called the Colorado Plateau, because corn would grow there.

The date was 1 A. D. or thereabouts. The character of the people is a little less certain but one thing is obvious, told by the earth itself. They did not originate there. These early inhabitants were immigrants, like the Spaniards, the English, the Germans, the Japs and the Chinamen who share the Pueblo country with them today. Like these others, they had come from the Old World to better their fortunes. However, it seems that in olden times, the flood of immigration moved not west but east. Instead of landing on the Atlantic coast, people then footed it up through Siberia and over Bering Strait, following the sloth, the mammoth, the camel, the bison and other animals now

2

extinct which represented their fortune—in other words, their food. We pause to ask how any one knows this and the answer is: from the earth itself. The earth of the Southwest, which carries so few roots of trees and grasses, is thick with scraps of broken pottery, old arrow points, bits of charred basketry, cloth and string. Until a few years ago it was thought legitimate fun and even business to delve among these things and findings were keepings. Now we know such vandalism to be as cruel as the tearing of a page from some irreplaceable book written five, seven, ten centuries ago.

It is a book in a nearly unknown language and the deciphering of it provides some of the most fascinating detective work now done. Here in a promising cave lie pots, made by Indians whom we know to be still living. Below are pots of other Indians now gone. So far the pottery specialist, laying aside the pieces one by one, can translate their record. But at last there is no more pottery. Earth! Ancient gravel which crumbled into place during centuries when this spot was unvisited, so the physicist says. *And then perhaps a bone, or even a whole skeleton.* Here the paleontologist must be called in and what excitement if he pronounces it that of an animal now vanished from the earth, one of those awkward giants which early man trapped in pits that he might have food! There may be other bones of other giants and, occasionally, one of those high moments when a new page is added to history—a layer of black charcoal. The uninitiated might shovel it away as only darker dirt but the digger knows that only one animal ever left burnt embers behind him and that is man. So man passed this way! Passed when the ancient animals of the ice age were

3

still alive and when a certain kind of gravel was crumbling into shape!

So the record is read and its bearing is this: all the early inhabitants of the New World, no matter how early, were immigrants. There is no sign of their fumbling for tools or learning to stand upright. They came full fledged bringing their tools with them. Asia, where much that is human seems to have started, may well have been their starting point, and indeed, the American Indians have *the straight black hair, high cheekbones, slanting eyes,* brownish skin and other features that are *called Mongolian.* They did not all come from one part of Asia and, even in those early days, there was no pure race. Men had already wandered and mixed along the shores of the Pacific, down into Africa and out into wild Europe. Those who pushed north through desolate Siberia, then south again where the ice would let them through, were men of different languages, different physiques and temperaments, and so are the American Indians. To speak of them all together, without any further classification, is like talking of *the* European, which might mean Englishman, Russian or Turk.

Nor did they come all at once. The pioneers who followed the melting ice ten or fifteen thousand years ago must have been far ahead of the next group. With them we have little to do for it is only on the edges of the Southwest that their caves and camping grounds are found. The story of our own region skips ten thousand years, with that light-heartedness which archaeology must learn, and brings us to the beginning of the Christian era and to that stretch of open country between the Rockies and the Sierras called the Great Basin.

4

...brilliantly colored figures .... with bright headbands over .... hair cut across the forehead like that of a mediæval page.

That country lies near the direct highway which the early travelers took down through the Yukon and Mackenzie valleys. It is a good place for hunters of simple tastes for, although there is never very much of any one kind of food, there is always something. The Paiute Indians lived on it, almost up to yesterday, hunting the rabbits that leaped between the sage brush, searching for berries, pine nuts and acorns, and shaking seeds for their flour from dozens of plants which modern farmers call weeds.

Someone was living in that very Basin just before 1 A.D. and living no doubt much as the Paiute did. Perhaps those early westerners spoke a language from the great group to which the Paiute belongs, an ancient and far flung group, stretching along the backbone of America from Idaho nearly to Mexico City. People of that group must have been a long time on the continent to work out so many different languages. Finding the likenesses between French, English and German is child's play compared to doing the same with these, yet there are likenesses. The ancestors of this huge spread of people must once have lived together when their grammar developed in common.

We have a guess at people who spoke a Uto-Aztecan language, like the Aztecs, the Hopi, the Mission Indians and hundreds of others in that north and south line that follows the backbone of the continent. Before 1 A.D. we only guess at what they could have been doing but after 1 A.D.—speaking in large round figures—they had corn. The discovery of the steam engine or of that far famed cotton jenny that industrialized England were not more epoch making. With corn Southwest history really begins. Trails are gradually being traced

5

←— The answer is corn.

through Mexico, Texas and the Mississippi Valley to learn where that corn came from. Surely it did not originate in this arid country where there is no wild plant anything like it. Its use was learned by these simple wanderers from some people which had developed it through centuries of patient toil. Since no one knows yet who those people were, we must leave a gap in the present story, a gap full of fascination for continued research. The people got corn and the tale, as after an act of magic, proceeds at different tempo.

So far we may watch the wandering seed gatherers raise more and more corn and finally Indian beans. We may see them move on to the Pueblo plateau where life would have been impossible without Mother Corn. They begin to build houses which have at first merely a circular cellar with a few feet of outside wall and a roof of poles and earth. We see how the untiring urge of the human race for craft led them to weave the only material they had, the twigs and leaves of the tough vegetation, into beautiful and complicated baskets for their household utensils. Preserved in the dry caves of the Southwest, these baskets have come down to us and given their owners the title of Basketmakers.

They must have flourished in the early years of the Christian era, while the Roman empire was growing and declining and while some of the Britons, whose descendants were to be among the later immigrants to America, were living in huts little better than those of the Basketmakers. We can picture these Basketmakers in loin cloths or scanty skirts, accompanied by the little dogs whose bones can still be found. They wore beautifully woven sandals, wrapped themselves in robes made of rabbit skin strips and carried woven bags. We

6

find their rough fields, their storage pits and the beginning of pottery. We can guess that they held some of the beliefs which seem most profoundly rooted in the Southwest: the belief that he who stays too near the dead is likely to be sucked somehow into the other world; the belief that supernatural power is evil as well as good and that the magician who cures can turn around and kill; the feeling that the worst fault in the world is to offend a neighbor. Such guesses can never be substantiated, for the Basketmakers were overwhelmed by floods of later immigrants. Not one new strain but many must have mixed and interbred, for so the unearthed skeletons proclaim. Perhaps it was that very mixture which gave the impetus to growth, as mixture has so often done in human history.

About 400 A.D. the immigration that was to give a new turn to life in the Southwest began. The earthern history uncovered by the diggers shows us the Basketmakers with their long skulls and throwing spears and beside them another race with round skulls and bows and arrows. Where did they come from? We find the trail here, lose it again there where it dips into the earth it taking with the mystery we seek to unravel, but it appears again to show that they brought with them the cotton which grows in the south. In the Pueblos of today we find parallel after parallel with ancient Mexico. Somewhere there is close connection between the great civilization of middle America and these northern cities, but it is involved, not so simple as a mere migration, all at once and in only one direction. With these newcomers we enter the last phase of Southwest history and reach that built by the ancient Pueblo people.

7

The detective processes of archaeology can follow step by step the way the new, mixed race gave up the little round pit house of the Basketmakers with its walls of poles thatched with brush, and the way they began to lay up stone to make square houses above ground. The ruins of such houses look tiny when we come upon a patchwork of them on some forgotten hillside but after the brush huts they must have seemed like mansions. The whole Southwest is peppered with them and its earth is littered with the scraps of pottery thrown out by their inhabitants. Each locality had its own design, held to as conservatively as a coat of arms. The movement of the people as they carried their design to a new locality where the clay and the style were different, produced a new style as identifiable as a grafted plant. In fact, the names of Southwest pottery remind one of botany, and the tyro hardly knows whether he is hearing a plant called Pluchea sericea, Nutt, or a scrap of broken pot called Hawikuh, Polychrome (Hargrave). Still, it is from the painstaking study of pottery, a science in itself, that the movements of the ancient Pueblo peoples have been established, step by step.

Recently too, the study of pottery has been aided by a new science. Since 1927 there has appeared a way for dating ancient ruins never before thought of: nature, it seems, keeps a record of climatic changes in the growth of trees. Every year the pine trees of the Southwest add a ring to their circumference; a wide ring if there has been plenty of rain, a narrow one if there has been little and sometimes none at all. The sequences of wide and narrow are the same for all pines with the same exposure over a two hundred mile area and by comparing the

8

first rings of a recent tree with the last rings of an older tree which grew on the same kind of slope one can establish a pictorial record of the years. Such a record has already been extended far beyond that of any living tree, back through the beams found in older and older houses to 700 A.D. Any ruin built after that year can be dated by the beams in its houses, or even by their scraps and the charcoal. With tree rings, pots and assorted rubbish, we can tell something about where and when the different peoples went. Sometimes we can tell why.

The record says that the small square houses of the pueblo people, standing in the high open places, began to draw together. It was found that a wall could be made to do double duty if several of the one-room houses were joined in a solid block. Perhaps too there were other immigrants coming down the plateau and the solid block helped with defense. They gathered closer and closer and the great epoch of the Pueblos began.

Its theatre was the Four Corners, a locality which means as much to Southwestern archaeology as the Nile to the ancient world and which appears on the map as the neatly ruled corners of four states, Utah, Colorado, Arizona and New Mexico. They join in a country of hill and canyon that is now desert except in Colorado, and a forbidding desert at that, but in the days the tree rings record, before man cut off the forests and man's cattle continued the destruction, there were living streams there. It was beside these streams, in sheltered canyons, that the great Pueblo houses were built.

Anyone who takes the desert drive to Chaco canyon in New Mexico will see the most amazing ruins in America. *These house ruins are now some rods from a wound in the earth called an arroyo* which must once have been a turbulent stream alive the whole year round. The archaeologist has evidence that this was so in the ceilings and roofs of the large buildings. As main supports there were beams a foot in diameter and the detective who seeks the clue to the old environment believes the pines of which they were hewn grew not far from the Pueblo, for he says they had no transportation scars as they would surely have had had they been carried a long distance like the beams of the church at Acoma. *We may think of the bare mesa behind the pueblo* which shows as a perpendicular and colorful backdrop of cliff *as having been as well wooded as some of the mountain tops of today.*

Crosswise of the beams, reeds and willows, plants which must have a great deal of water, which in fact grow in the water, were placed in regular rows and lavishly, so that one cannot help but conclude that they were plentiful. If there was a large supply of water we can easily understand why this valley may have been chosen by the great apartment house builders. Today water is scarce and alkaline. The once living river has become a dry bed of terrifying proportions. During the rainy season vast quantities of water pour down it carrying with them permanent destruction, for they cut the soil away depositing it eventually where the river quiets down. In a few hours all is dry again and the earth is left sharply lacerated. The wealth of life-giving water comes too fast to soak in; soil, rocks, and such trees as were left in its path have no way but to go with it, in their turn aiding the cutting.

Along the arroyo in ten miles of narrow valley were thirty large apartment houses each one a village. Their shape was like an amphitheater with every seat a room. Facing south to get the sun, their backs to the canyon wall, they rose from a height of one room at the front to three, four and five at the back. Pueblo Bonito, one of the large ones, could accommodate a thousand people, and, until the building of skyscrapers began about fifty years ago, it was the largest apartment house in the world.

Not all the rooms could be lived in. The bottom ones at the back, which had no chance for light and air, were used for storage while the families lived in the upper rooms, each using as balcony and dooryard the roof of the lower tier in front. In those days openings were few and entrances were often square hatchways in the roof, reached by ladders made of notched poles. We marvel at thought of the sandalled housewife, a jar of water from the river on her head, climbing the notched pole, or perhaps a series of notched poles to the roof of her house and descending the pole to its floor. We know that *the woman* even in those early days *plastered the house as does her descendant today,* for she left her fingermarks here and there in the clay.

One room in such a house was the dwelling for a family; the stove a pit in the floor; the chimney, the hatchway. *In the court in front* corresponding to the stage of the amphitheatre, *were sunk the great windowless rooms which the Spaniards called estufas, or stoves.* Probably they were warm in winter but also cool in summer and they served the year round as lodges in which men took council and communed with the spirits. Actually, they were nothing more than the pit houses of earlier days, larger and more elaborate, with formal

11

arrangements whose use we can now only guess at. Everyone has noticed how, for sacred things, people cling to the old fashions which have been hallowed, as modern churches so long clung to the great silver communion cup. So the pueblo people, though they had learned to live above ground, never abandoned the sunken room for their altars. Kiva, the Hopi word, has become the white man's name for it.

When present-day Hopi men prepare a ceremony in kiva, they unbind their long hair and, wearing only a loincloth, squat to smoke and spread the cornmeal for the supernaturals. Perhaps it was done thus in the ancient pueblos. Outside, the younger men, in loincloths and sandals, would be digging the fields with a sharp stick. The women would sit on the roofs at their pottery and basketry, in robes of black cotton, woven for them by the men and worn, like a scanty Roman toga, under the left arm and fastened on the right shoulder. Perhaps a dance went on in the plaza, with women in snow white mantles or men in fearsome masks and trappings of spruce boughs.

This great period of the ancient Pueblos was from about 900 to 1300 A.D., the time when the first great cathedrals were being built in Europe. We can follow ruin by ruin the building of *the great apartment houses* in Chaco canyon. Two of them, Pueblo Bonito and Chettro Ketl, *can still be seen, almost completely unearthed. Others with their well-preserved masonry, oddly-shaped doorways, curved kiva walls, holes through which beams once protruded, and in cases, even the beams themselves,* are in process of excavation. Long before 1300 the whole canyon was abandoned and the building urge went elsewhere.

Enemies caused the change. These city dwellers had crowded into

12

And then perhaps a bone, or even a whole skeleton. —→

These house ruins are now some rods from a wound in the earth called an arroyo...

⟵ *. . . . the straight black hair, high cheekbones, slanting eyes . . . . called Mongolian.*

the great houses and canyons for protection and their very danger had inspired the building of the amazing dwellings, but even *with their blank rear walls for defense and with lookout towers* scattered down the valley they were not safe. Hordes of strangers must have been entering from north and west because the pueblo dwellers moved east, but not at first. The great period went on in another part of the Four Corners, Mesa Verde in Colorado. Here was a really well protected place *where the apartment houses went up in shelf-like caves,* scoured by the wind high up in sandstone cliffs. When these dwellings were first discovered they were attributed to a vanished race of giants or magicians. Now the study of pots and tree rings makes their story plain. They were community dwellings, occupied a little longer than those of New Mexico and deserted at the time that the tree rings show a great drought, at the end of the 13th century. Last refuge near the Four Corners was in the northern deserts of Arizona along the Little Colorado River, not far from where the Hopi are now. *Here* in the most picturesque caves of all, shadowed like huge proscenium arches, *crouch the latest community dwellings, smaller and much less carefully built than the tiered amphitheatres* of the Chaco but weird and striking beyond all the others.

All the villages of the Four Corners were deserted by 1300 and the white men were not to come until 250 years later. They did not cause the builders of the great houses to discard their striking architectural scheme or the potters to degenerate from their former precise beauty. The tree rings tell us of a drought which must have kept the cornfields of Mesa Verde barren for twenty-three years. Where the

13

←— We may think of the bare mesa behind the pueblo .... as having been as well wooded as some of the mountain tops today.

drought did not reach, there were enemies, breaking up the great pueblo civilization, and causing the people to move and move again. That danger was from Indians, some of them the Ute, at the north and west, and Comanche at the east. Later the foreign Navajo and Apache did their part. There was little destruction. The great urge for building and for craft which had flowered so spontaneously seems to have died without the application of outward force. Something else was in the minds of the pueblo builders. They moved away while the European Renaissance was beginning and after 1500, let us say, they no longer built great houses.

This decline and fall, so dimly pictured, is one of the most interesting events in history and we can surmise an economic basis for it. People were moving in small groups intent only on keeping alive. They joined any other group they could and the village unity, the village craft, was dissipated. For the student of art this is an unimportant interlude; for the student of American history it has great significance. It was the time when the great region of the Pueblos shrank to three score of villages or only twice as many as there are today. For every village existing at the present time, the diggers say there are scores of ruins. The last villages shrank to the east as though danger had been in the west. We find them still in a thin west and east line from Hopi in Arizona to the Rio Grande in New Mexico and a little way up and down the Rio Grande. Their territory kept on shrinking, even in Spanish days.

We are interested not only in where the Pueblos got to during that blank transition time but in who got to them. When we look at the

Pueblos now, we find four language families, utterly different and each, except Zuni, with several dialects. One of them is Hopi, belonging to the Shoshonean, or more broadly speaking Uto-Aztecan, language group which we have already mentioned. Hopi might be guessed to go back to the very beginning of pueblo history, but Zuni has no obvious relatives anywhere and the relatives of the others are being surmised far to the south and east. So far we cannot trace the mingling of these peoples who must have had, not only different languages, but different governments, different religions. Some came in at the great break when long-headed people gave place to round-headed, and throwing spear to bow and arrow. Others probably came in the Pueblo "dark ages" when the builders of the great houses picked up their belongings and moved east. To unravel that history is not impossible, and while it is being done we can look at the Pueblo Indians as that most stimulating of human phenomena, a mixture of breed and customs.

In 1540 they were found by Coronado, marching his men across the Southwest in search of gold. It was a heartbreaking expedition for the Conquistadores, trailing over the sun baked plains in their leathern hauberks with their horses dropping of thirst, to be butchered by the wandering Indians. The tale of that disappointment, which revealed only villages and cornfields instead of gold, has often been told. For the Spaniards it was one more expedition; for the Indians, the beginning of a new era. Sixty years later New Mexico was part of the Spanish dominions. A royal decree commanded that each Indian village, no matter what its own system of government had been, should elect a governor and lieutenant governor to carry out Spanish in-

15

structions. Franciscan priests appeared, gently urging the natives to build churches and appointing native church officers to see to the tithes and the services, forbidding the old rituals as of the devil. Spanish beads, silver and copper, began to take their place among native treasures. Spanish soldiers found native mates.

It was not a mere conquest, for the old civilization was too tough and too deeply rooted. In fact for a while it seemed that the Pueblos would throw out the invaders altogether. Ninety years after the occupation they rose, murdered their priests, and kept every Spaniard out of the country for thirteen years, but Spain came back. Soldiers, priests, governors, merchants—there were too many of them to keep out, and the strong old Indian culture slowly adapted itself. The villages accepted their governors, at least in New Mexico, for Arizona was too wild and distant to be included. Eastern towns acquired the saints' names by which they are known today, most of them keeping their old names only in their own language. They accepted priest and church and this does not mean that they gave lip service only. One who has seen a modern ceremony, where the saint is carried into the plaza to watch the pagan dancing, must admit that the combination is much more intricate than that. Perhaps Catholicism was admitted at first as a new form of magic to be practised alongside the old and to add to its power. In time the sprinkling of cornmeal and the sign of the cross came to have equal value; funeral and marriage became essential, Christianity was an integral part of the life in many pueblos.

This does not mean that it was Christianity exactly as the priests

16

or as the later missionaries have taught it. Christianity has undergone many interpretations since it was preached by Jews to Romans and by Romans to Goths and Britons. Each group of converts has added to the religion some color and form out of its own past, and the Pueblo Indians did also. They received Christianity as it was preached in Spain in the seventeenth century. They added to it the dance and the drama which constitute their own religious ceremony, and they made a compound which is as true for them as the special combination of hymns and prayers which are hallowed by the White are for him. At some of their ceremonies one sees more of ancient Spain than persists in Spain itself, with a color and tempo that are truly Pueblo.

The Spaniards brought more than their religion. Pueblo people watching from their remote settlements helped themselves one by one to those importations which seemed to them useful. Horses and cattle were a revelation since they had no domestic animals or beasts of burden. Most pueblos now have horses, sheep and goats. They learned to raise Spanish wheat and also kidney beans, peas, melons, cabbages, onions, apples, and peaches. They liked the hive shaped oven which the early Spaniards built and hardly a pueblo village is now to be seen without a group of these seventeenth century novelties. *The Spaniards had learned from the Moors to use a chimney, and the observant pueblo people copied it, using a pile of bottomless pots.* There were chimneys in the pueblos while villages in the British Isles were still without them. Clothing too was accepted by the pueblo people, though their men up to now had found a loincloth sufficient. Their country was often cold and the intricately sewed sleeves and trousers of the foreigners had advantages. However, the people of Taos to this day cut the seat from trousers, to make them as much like the old leggings as possible, and wear special herbs in moccasins.

Such were the changes brought by the Spaniards, some of them as many as four hundred years ago. With them they brought hostility too and a sense that questions asked by the white man and proposals made by him bode no good. The ancient societies that wished to keep their own ways had to fight, not openly but quietly, with a wall of smiling defense. They were not equipped to argue in the white man's languages that the way which had kept them peaceful and prosperous for so many centuries might still be the best way—for them. They simply retired behind the walls of dwellings and sacred houses. Secrecy, which may not have been one of their characteristics in olden times, became an outstanding one. No white man perhaps understands the eternal vigilance which must be taught even in early childhood to guard sacred customs from ridicule and interference.

Spain weakened, Spain gave way, and in 1821 the pueblos found themselves part of the Republic of Mexico. Perhaps no one has realized how different might have been their development had the United States not needed their country and if it had not very quickly obtained it, for Mexico had no Indian reservations or Indian wards. According to her constitution: "All residents of the republic shall have equal rights in voting and office holding, without regard to race or color." Of course all were taxed too. That principle has held, at least in theory, for a hundred years, and perhaps as a result, it would be hard to find anywhere in Mexico a ceremony or a government so

18

completely Indian as some of those in the United States. The advantage, or the loss, caused by that determined amalgamation is a subject for long discussion, but it seems likely that, without the treaty of Guadalupe Hidalgo, the pueblos might well have ceased to be such islands of picturesque native life as they are now.

That treaty was made in 1848 and the United States confirmed to Mexican citizens in the newly acquired land all the property and rights which they had enjoyed under Mexico. That meant, in the first place, that the pueblos received title to their land, not as a reservation assigned them on government domain, but as their own property. Spain had given them such titles long ago, some even before the pueblo rebellion, most when the frightened government, expelled for twelve years to Texas, was making gestures of generosity. The United States confirmed the holdings as well as they could be worked out from old records.

The pueblos had status as property holders, unlike that of any other Indians, but the new government, fresh from its wars with the wild Indians of the plains, had no idea with what a civilized people it was dealing. The right to vote and to hold office seemed quite beside the question, and the Supreme Court ruled that the pueblos were, like the conquered nomads, "domestic dependent nations, in a state of pupilage". The territory of New Mexico legislated that they had no right to vote, and, as the new country got organized, the Indian Office took over the wardship of the pueblos and their lands.

"A more upright and honest people," said their first agent, "are nowhere to be found. ....I can but recommend them and their possessions to the protection and fostering hand of the government. They are a loyal people and richly deserving of our sympathy. ... Give them some money for tools and some proper teaching and in ten years they will hold their own with the rest of the country."

The tools were forthcoming ultimately, and the Pueblos gladly took them. Then there were a few schools and a friendly recognition by a distant chief called Abraham Lincoln who sent to each governor and lieutenant governor a cane of office with Lincoln's name on a silver disc. The independent little city states received these gestures with friendliness and they helped the new government when it needed guides and even fighters. Amalgamation was another matter. As the new towns grew and the railroads came, the pueblo people padded, in their beautifully made moccasins, on the outskirts of this activity, watching and trading and taking only what seemed to them truly useful. The rest they left to white men.

The white men took their duties seriously and their first thought, after an Indian Office had been properly organized, was that the Pueblos would want to change their ways as soon as possible. It could be done in one generation was the conviction. Take the young ones away to boarding school, immerse them in white ways, and keep them so. They will come back converted and they will convert their villages. The immensity of this plan as one sees it worded simply and nobly in the dedications of the old schools partakes of a belief in magic. No one dreamed in those days but that civilizations were arranged in a regular scale from the most primitive up to the highest and that anyone would be glad to take a step up. Two if possible. The pueblo children,

. . . .the woman. . . .plastered the house as does her descendant today. . . .

In the court in front were sunk the great windowless rooms which the Spaniards called estufas or stoves.

....the great apartment houses ....can still be seen, almost completely unearthed.

Others with their well-preserved masonry, oddly-shaped doorways, curved kiva walls, holes through which beams once protruded and, in cases, even the beams themselves . . . .

however, offered their step up, seemed only to go off into space. They came home, not white, but merely perplexed and lonely, and sometimes they remained so all their lives. Now school is tried in another way.

Must there be school? Yes, the Pueblos want it. The white people are too thick around them. The stores, the trains, the machines are too much a part of their daily life. They want to know English. They want to run a car, use a sewing machine, and figure an account, just as in Spanish times they wanted to ride horses and plant wheat. If they did not do these things, their little islands of primitive life would become prisons, so there are day schools in the pueblos. They are run by the Indian Office and they are said to have the same grades and the same standards as a public school. White teachers are trying to fit the instruction given there to the Indian's world. Reading lessons describe, not fire engines in a city or the old oaken bucket on a New England farm, but the laying up of stones in a pueblo house. Practical work is the sewing, cooking, and building needed at the very spot. Children who finish the day school may go to high school, vocational school, and ultimately with a government loan, to college.

There are hospitals near the pueblos and anyone willing to try the white man's treatment may be taken there. There are men to teach about the care of cattle and to help in their sale. There are men to explain how the wasting and cutting of the soil, which must have begun before the white man came, has been increasing greatly since the pueblo people have pastured cattle around their villages. Most of the villages still have their old governments or those which they evolved under the Spanish rule. The land set aside for them is untaxed and they may use it singly or collectively as they wish. Their residents are wards of the United States who take part in managing their own governments but do not vote in the elections of the Whites unless they move from their lands and take out citizenship.

The lands, which have shaped the fate of these ancient villages, kept them settled, kept them peaceful, served as an interest in life through all vicissitudes—the lands are still the center of their existence. About 1924, however, the white government realized these lands seemed to be melting away. White settlers had been moving in ever since Spanish days, taking land and using water, until some pueblos could no longer make a living. The mills of government ground slowly but ground well, and as a result the Indians are getting either their land or an equivalent in money. Nineteen pueblos will have anywhere from three to one hundred eighty-eight thousand dollars apiece to spend on land, irrigation, and tools. Will this be the beginning of a modernization, not by law, but by the driving force of economics, as real as wind and rain?

For the present the Pueblos remain on the verge of the white man's world, dipping into it only occasionally. Point by point they decide whether they will accept the innovations around them, with full knowledge of how the smallest change may lead to another that finally undermines a total system. Wheat flour, they admit, is easier to come by than the cornmeal ground by a kneeling woman. Yet when the maiden no longer grinds, the youth no longer plays to her on the flute. When the Corn Mother is not the chief food, there is an end of that intricate system by which trays of cornmeal are interchanged as gifts. Perhaps, then, the obligations of kin go with it, for it is hard to find a gift of equal significance. The interlocking of all these parts that go to make the structure of their old civilization is known to the pueblo people, either consciously or unconsciously. That may be why a certain village forbids so strictly that there shall be white man's stoves in the sitting room, though they are allowed in the kitchen, and why wearing shoes instead of moccasins is also suspect.

The pueblos change slowly behind their walls of secrecy. Yet history shows they have always changed. No one can make them stand still, for no people has ever stood still. But as they move slowly out from their isolation they may bring to the life around them a new power and color. We shall have glimpses from a new angle altogether as to what constitutes happiness, work, government.

2

The Peaceful Hopi

When the girls at an Indian school give an ultra modern fashion show the spectator may pick out, among the shy mannequins with permanent waves, a neat figured maiden who wears her silk frock with an urban grace. She is a Hopi. At the great yearly ceremonial where the Southwest Indians give a version of some of their ceremonies as a spectacle for the Whites, one dancing group stands out for precision and finish. They are the Hopi. When somewhere in that close and friendly community which is the Southwest one hears of "an Indian" who is a skilled railroad hand, a deft waitress, a clever merchant, that craftsman is very likely to turn out a Hopi.

Yet the Hopi are the most remote from white civilization of all the pueblo dwellers and their barren mesas more than any other locality in the Southwest afford glimpses of the life of the ancient apartment houses. The Hopi are actually urban and have been urban for centuries. The gray stone houses just visible over the rim of Oraibi mesa represent the oldest continuously inhabited town in the United States. There a government has been functioning for at least four hundred years. There people have been living as close to one another as they do in any modern city and there they have developed the graciousness, the poise, the alertness as well as the reserve, which are called urban. If you have business dealings with a Hopi you will find him suavely competent at every point. If you dine or converse with him you will meet a smiling ease, an evasion of awkward topics which white Americans call Old World manners.

Hopituh means Peaceful Ones. That is not the sort of name most Indians give themselves, for generally a tribe simply calls itself *the people* as though the rest of the human race did not exist. If *people* is qualified at all it is by obvious geography like People of the River or the Mountain. A psychological distinction like Peaceful People argues a sophistication and a history.

The land of the Peaceful lies far north on the plateau of Arizona, the very country where the ancient pueblos were. Those pueblos are in ruins, roaming Navajo have filled the land, and still the Hopi perch there alone, the desert their protection. They are, however, no longer inaccessible. Though men and horses used to die of thirst traveling toward those mesas, automobiles carrying white men and Hopis now make the trip in half a day from the railroad. Turn off the highway and bounce through dry stream beds, over alkali flats and up slopes where the colored clays lie stratified like an earthen rainbow. Fifteen or twenty miles from the Hopi villages you begin to come upon cornfields, cuddled in the low places above underground water. The Hopi run to those cornfields every day in summer, but they do not move the villages nearer to them.

These still cling to the flat tops of the mesas which point south, three in a row, like peninsulas jutting into a sea of sand. First Mesa, Second Mesa, and Third Mesa, (counting from the east), the white men call them. Few can remember the chiming variations of the village names—Shungopovi, Spring where Narrow Reeds Grow; Walpi, Place of the Gap; Oraibi, the Rock. There are eleven of them in all. You may climb up by an automobile road, *pushing your car around rocky corners edged with sky*, or you may still take the old foot trail, pausing with madly pumping heart to *gaze out over the cloud-shadowed desert*, flecked as far as the eye can follow with the tiny patches of green which mark the Hopi cornfields. *At the base of the mesa you may note a spring with a tuft of evergreen planted by its brink.* The evergreen are tied with cotton, an offering to the clouds which it somewhat resembles. Farther on feathers peep from a cave, the haunt of some supernatural where rainwater stands in a sandstone hollow. Here the women come with gasoline cans which replace the ancient water jars, and *naked children find their one real bathtub* just as they must have found it in ancient times.

Your eyes come level with the mesa top and the gray unevenness which had seemed to be rock, resolves itself into clustered one-, two-, and three-storey houses, built of the same sandstone as the mesa itself. It seems more as if the rock had windows and doors than as though the houses were made by man; *for front yard there is a precipice dropping into the void.*

The house beside you may be a new one with bright painted door frames and glass windows, furnished with a blue enamel stove from the mail order house and dishes set on oilcloth-covered shelves made of orange crates. It may have an earthen floor spread with a sheepskin on which the family sit to dip together from the common pot.

You may talk to an old man in moccasins, velvet blouse and blanket, a queer combination of costume which the Hopi have learned through he years, moccasins from the Navajo or their kind, blouse from the Spaniards, blanket their own. He wears it with the ease of a race long accustomed to clothing and to walking carefully in houses, and he answers your questions with the self-possession of a perfect host.

"How did the Hopi come to live on these barren mesas?"

"They came here, clan by clan, after long wandering."

"Wandering from where?"

"From underground."

That is the answer of most Southwest Indians, and students have racked their brains as to whether underground means a cave, a dark place, a cold place, a warm place. Or has it no meaning? The Hopi themselves do not puzzle about that. They know that they lived in the lowest of four worlds underground and they climbed up, led by the war gods. Above, they met the skeleton god of death who owns the soil and they asked his permission to plant corn. They kept on planting in all their wanderings though there was a time when

28

....where the apartment houses went up in shelf-like caves....

The Spaniards had learned from the Moors to use a chimney, and the observant pueblo people copied it, using a pile of bottomless pots (San Ildefonso).

. . . . with their blank rear walls for defense and with lookout towers . . . .

Must there be school? Yes, the pueblos want it.

the Corn Maidens were offended and went away, to return again only for the summer months.

Hopi history begins with corn. What went before it? The pottery scraps tell us that there have been people living around the Hopi mesas for at least eight hundred years and more. The language places the Peaceful in that huge language stock of the Uto-Aztecan which includes many of the primitive seed gatherers. Were the Hopi a group of these who moved into the pueblo plateau and learned about corn, or was it the other way round? Did they gradually acquire city ways from the other residents? The Hopi still use flour from wild seeds on certain sacred occasions; they still keep and kill sacred eagles and bury them in a cemetery like the seed-gatherers to the west. In other important customs however and in their very physique, they are unlike these primitive kinsmen. They must have made the break a long time ago for, though we know the group their language belongs to, it stands alone within that group. And the Hopi stand alone among pueblo peoples. Remote on their mesas, beyond the scope of white influence till a few years ago, keepers of the old customs, they may well be the oldest and first of pueblo dwellers.

They are the only pueblo people still living in the land where the great apartment houses flourished in the past, and there seems to be a reason for that. Their mesas are in inaccessible country and they have the only permanent water for miles around. Not streams which dry up upon occasion, but springs which bubble from under the rock at the edge of the cliffs even more willingly in dry seasons than in wet. Those springs are sacred to the Hopi and woe to the sanitation expert who plans to clean and pipe the shrine where the priests plant their prayersticks. Water to the Hopi is blessed and holy in a way that only desert people can understand.

People lived around this water from at least 1150 A. D., or even before. They did not live on the mesas in those early days for they seem to have moved up later because of fear. At the mesa foot they had built their huts of logs carried from the nearby mountains. Here they planted corn, even after a volcano had covered some of the country with ash, and here they made beautiful pottery fired in a coal kiln. Yes, coal! It is only coarse lignite but the Hopi found it in the sandstone and mined it. They and the English, says one of the students who discovered this, were the only two peoples who found out independently that black rocks would burn.

Then came the great and flaming date for the Southwest, 1540. The Spaniards! The people of the now ruined village of Hawikuh near Zuni would not let them in. It is said they even strewed cornmeal across the trail for that was their ceremonial sign to keep out intruders. The Spianards disregarded the cornmeal and destroyed the town. Then the other villages sued for peace.

With that very first overture, the Peaceful had established their method of combatting the white invader. It was passive resistance. In the middle of a desert where the conquerors could reach them only by days of thirsty traveling the Hopi remained polite. It is true that priests finally came but the Hopi poisoned only one of them, bearing with others for some thirty years. In 1680 the rebellion came when all the pueblos acted together for the one time in history, and succeeded in driving out the Spaniards. The Hopi did their part by killing their four priests and after that no priests ever came to stay again. It is said that the Hopi got together and destroyed one of their own villages which had allowed its people to be baptised, but historians have killed that story. They admit however, that the Hopi once sent ambassadors to Santa Fe with the proposal to Spain: "Let us have a truce, you to keep your religion, we to keep ours."

Spain was not cooperative and the Hopi moved up on the mesas. In the days of attacks by roving nomads, only Oraibi had been aloft while the other towns had defended themselves from the valley. Now they had to get as far as possible from the new invaders, and they thought they could do this by going up. They even invited some distant pueblo people to come and camp on guard at the head of the trail up First Mesa. So the Hano came from the Rio Grande country and are still there. The story says: The Hopi said to the Hano: "We will spit in your mouths and then you can speak our language. Then you spit in our mouths and we will speak yours." The Hopi spat but he Hano did not and the Hopi has never learned to talk Hano.

Those years after the Spaniards came back were dark ages for the pueblos. The white men had brought horses and the wild, roaming tribes took to them as though they had been riders in some previous incarnation. They could now go everywhere and the cornfields and storage bi ns of the villagers attracted them most. Navajo, Ute, Apache, Comanche streamed over the land and the pueblo people simply moved out. Some founded new villages farther east; some took refuge with the Hopi; some even joined the invaders and the small, compact physique of their descendants may perhaps still be identified in a rangy Navajo throng.

Alone in a devastated area the Hopi held out. They had been quite willing to learn from the Spanish fathers how to plant peach trees, watermelons and other European vegetables, and to raise sheep. They had their springs, but there were dreadful times when all the water failed and the population died off from seven thousand to seven hundred. Nevertheless, when the Spanish governor offered them a wagonload of food, the starving town of Oraibi refused it. They had nothing to give in return they said.

Spain became too feeble to do much about the Hopi and when Mexico got her independence, she did nothing at all, barring making a few raids for slaves. The Hopi were left to the mercy of the Navajo. Visitors who see the two groups hobnobbing peacefully on one reservation and who ask if they speak the same language, are unaware that the reservation is Hopi land, preempted by the intruders. They may not have heard the story that the Hopi finally captured some Navajo and brought them home to feast. As the Navajo squatted on the floor to eat, a woman with a heavy grinding stone in her hand stood behind each of them. At a signal, the grinding stones came down and smashed the heads of the Navajo. Or that of the Navajo, who were feasted in the most urbane fashion, and, after the meal, hurled unceremoniously over the cliffs.

The Navajo were dealt with by the white men whom they annoyed

32

even more than they had the Hopi. Somehow unnoticed by the pueblo people, Mexico had had a war with a new country called the United States, and as a result, New Mexico and Arizona had become one of its territories. Pioneers, taking possession of the country, complained about the Navajo and Apache, the pioneers who had immediately preceded them. The marauding became worse and worse and little Kit Carson in his fur cap was sent out to take measures. Kit was not literary, but he could subdue Indians. Once when he was commanded to subdue a whole tribe he noted the fact in his diary: "Done so." He "done so" with the Navajo to the extent of driving the whole tribe miles and miles and imprisoning them at Ft. Sumner in Texas. Ultimately the Hopi as well as the Whites got some peace but for a long time after the United States thought everything was settled, roving bands continued to make the desert dangerous for travelers. It was hard on the Hopi, who not only had to fight their own battles, but were even treated by the Whites as though they too were roving bandits.

At least they did not have to fight the influence of white civilization. While the other Pueblos were changing more rapidly than was good for them, the Hopi, thanks to their enemies, the Navajo, were kept isolated as as if in quarantine. The desert had kept the Spaniards away; the pioneers who were toughened to the desert minded the Navajo but not for long. White civilization was spreading as rapidly as water from a leak. A railroad was put through to the south of the Hopi, the Navajo quieted down, Arizona became a state and set up an Indian agency; a Protestant missionary appeared on Third Mesa and stayed, the United States

33

government took charge of the Indians and proposed sending all Hopi children to boarding school.

The notion brought about civil war in the veteran town of Oraibi which had gone its own way since 1120. The conservatives refused to let their children go; the progressives approved, they decided to settle it by a tug of war in which the progressives won. The conservatives, being poor losers, moved further along the mesa, taking with them some of the sacred paraphernalia and some of the priests, and founded a town called Hotevilla. From that moment Oraibi began to die. Eight hundred years it had existed, inhabited all that time, for all we know, by people of the same race who still go up and down between its little stone houses. They had resisted battle from race after race, but they could not resist school.

At present all Hopi children go to school and apparently like it. The government set aside the land around them which at first they had shared unwillingly with their old enemies, the Navajo, as a reservation. The Hopi grumbled, but little by little the two people became more friendly. One who sees the Navajo now, crowding to the Hopi Snake Dance, must admit that they seem as welcome as—the Whites. The Hopi are smilingly gracious to all and take out their iritation in quiet grumbling among themselves. The Navajo in their turn look down upon the Hopi for "they are not brave, nor are they good horsemen."

At Keam's Canyon, thirteen miles east of First Mesa, there is a hospital where all Hopis who trust the white man's medicine may be treated free. There is a field nurse resident on Second Mesa, and

34

a doctor who makes regular visits. These medical people have their own problem in preventing the spread of trachoma and other new diseases while the Hopi insist upon living on mesas where a sewage system is plainly impossible. On or near each mesa at a respectful distance from the villages is a day school with laundry, sewing room and carpenter shop, in some cases with a community house. The more up-to-date they are the better the Hopi like them. Idealistic young teachers eager to get close to the primitive, instead find themselves furnishing modern recipes and helping to write the mail orders from the catalogue.

The Hopi are craftsmen and, when they see a chance for a new technique, they take it. They started a community house recently, and white people watched with interest what they thought would be the construction of a genuine old pueblo dwelling. Instead they saw a modern building, its stones as neatly cut as those of a new post office.

"But," said the Hopi, "we have iron tools now. Of course we cut our stones even."

Of course also, they buy automobiles when they can, or at least horses and wagons. They have little gardens at the mesa foot for chili, beans and onions, but they also keep sheep to sell, and their young men go off to work on government roads and in railroad yards, their girls to housework. The Hopi have realized that money is useful, but all these competent workers flock back for the initiation in the fall and the farewell to the dancing gods in midsummer. Even those who are making the best pay plan to retire ultimately to the mesa top where there are no modern improvements.

35

Upon that mesa top the houses are still built along a line of corn-meal strewed with prayer, and from the rafters hang feathers, offer-ings for rain and blessing. The babies born within them are presented to the sun at dawn, after the house has been strewed with cornmeal and the gleaming black hair of the mother has been washed in yucca root which served the Indian before soap was known and which makes a more satifsactory shampoo than any commercial hair emulsion. The dreadful magic of birth has previously been removed by dusting the baby with ashes, a method of discharming not appreciated by white nurses.

Many mothers still use the cradleboard, on which the solemn-eyed baby is strapped, acquiring a straight back and a calm demeanor for the future. The baby leaves it when he is able to walk, and walking seems not at all delayed because there has been little chance to kick. His little brown body seems as straight and healthy as though he exercised every day. In other days he would have played about naked up to the time of adolescence, but *now he may have clothes from the mail order house* or at least from his mother's sewing machine. By six he may be in school, learning earnestly to say:

I have a little blue chair at school

I like to sit in my little blue chair.

By eight he should be initiated into Hopi village life. There come to visit the mesas every year, in the months from April to August, certain mysterious beings who bring the rain, in fact, *are* the rain. With bare torsos and embroidered kilts such as the ancient Hopi used to wear, they dance in the plazas in strange masks, and the Hopi call

36

.... pushing your car around rocky corners edged with sky.... ⟶

....*to gaze out over the cloud-shadowed desert*....

them kachinas. That they are the men of the village marvelously costumed is known to all adults, but a child takes his first step into the common life when this fact is revealed to him. It happens when he is somewhere near eight years old and when his chosen godfather takes him into the kiva to meet the gods face to face.

After initiation come the years *when Hopi children play* by helping their elders. It is the "activity" training found in the most modern schools but it goes them one better, for here no one has to think up interesting tasks for the children to do. There are plenty of tasks right in the family, and even a baby's work really helps. Five or ten miles the little boy follows his father to the cornfield where the colored corn stands in separate rows, white, yellow, blue, red, purple and mixed. There grow the little Indian beans that have been raised since Basketmaker times, the squash, the oil-giving sunflower and the white man's chili and watermelons. He fetches firewood from the mountains and, though he no longer uses bow and arrow, he joins the men when they go out with their curved sticks for the village rabbit hunt.

The girl makes the wafer bread whose thin, folded sheets look like a blue or pink wasp's nest. For ceremonial occasions she grinds the corn, kneeling to push her cylindrical grinding stone up and down, up and down, over a granite slab called the metate. *It takes hours to grind first on the coarse slab*, then on the finer, then on the finest of all, till the cornmeal is light as powder, but a girl who can not do it is not fit to marry.

If the mother is a craftswoman she teaches her daughter to make

37

baskets or pots as the case may be. Residence decides. *If she lives on First Mesa, she will make pottery* with a background of variegated orange like a morning cloud and decorations in red and black. On Second Mesa she will make basketry trays of thick spiral coils. *The hardest part of the tray is to get it started,* and once a number of centers is on hand the women of the family can go on with the work quite rapidly. *The mother will have a bee at which many of her friends make centers.* They will all feast with her on roast mutton and corn, and each will later have a bee of her own to get *her* centers started. On Third Mesa she will make her trays of wickerwork, with striking designs of eagles, squash blossoms or swirls. *When you buy one of these products of Hopi craft, a wastepaper basket for example, you will know it comes from Third Mesa.*

Yet the specification was established accidentally and not too long ago. It is an example of the way taboos and customs grow up and flourish in Hopiland, in the Tyrol, and in many other villages of the world. All the Hopi used once to make pottery, and the diggers can recite its progress and its changes of style. Most women still can make rough kitchen utensils but the lovely decorated jars grew less perfect as the Spaniards and the other Whites brought in their wares. Forty years ago decorated pottery was already on its way out.

It was at that time that diggers came to Hopi and began to excavate one of the ancient villages. The Peaceful watched and listened with interest as the white men explained to them the beautiful arts of their own ancestors, and a woman took fire from that explanation. Hopi women have always been the potters, and Nampeyo of Walpi, looking at the ancient designs, felt an artist's urge to copy them. She did so for thirty years, even when she was going blind, and she became one of the outstanding artists among American Indians. It is because of her that the women of First Mesa now make their beautiful pots. They make them for sale, not for use. White women delight to have them for ornament while the Hopi women keep water in a metal container.

Basketry never lost its beauty for it was too closely interwoven with Hopi ceremonies, but the old wealth of mats and strainers and other household baskets diminished until now the Hopi make for their own use only basketry trays. Never say that Indians do not change. Second Mesa still uses the old spiral coils that date from Basketmaker times while Third Mesa picked up wickerwork only a few hundred years ago. However with both of them trays are still the only thing in which sacred cornmeal can be carried.

Corn to the Hopi is the symbol of life, and corn thrice ground is the perfect food, perfectly prepared. Before ceremonies the women relatives of the performers can be seen padding through the streeet in little moccasins (or once in a while on high-heeled slippers) carrying trays of blue or pink cornmeal. There is a woman's society which dances in the autumn in honor of food and harvest and throws among the crowd beautifully designed corn trays for the young men to struggle for. The most imposing tray the Hopi make is the extra-sized one which Second Mesa heaps with meal ground by a bride and gives to her husband's relatives. It is carried triumphantly in the wedding procession and the legend is that when the husband dies and his spirit steps into the air at the rim of the Grand Canyon, it is this basket tray which will waft him down to the Hopi land of the dead.

We have seen that two of the most famous Hopi arts belong to women, and when we study a beautiful basket or pot we can never say "The artist, he. . . ."; but men have an unexpected art, weaving. The "distaff side" of the family has always been the male side with the Peaceful whose men cannot, in recent years, have been preoccupied with war and hunting. They had time to raise cotton and to spin it on a long stick with weighted end, although now they buy yarn from the store. A few old men still squat before their upright looms, fixed to two posts in the house floor. Generally it is the kiva floor, since the kiva has more room, and so it must have been from ancient times, for ruined kivas show the same two post holes. Slowly working from the bottom up, they fabricate the white dancing kilts with darkly striking borders which might almost be embroidery; the scant black dresses for women, worn with one shoulder out, one shoulder in; the fringed white ceremonial sashes; and the girls' white bridal robes and mantles. None of these things is worn in daily life except the woman's dress, but for the religious ceremonies when long lines of dancers stamp the earth in honor of the supernaturals, the ancient costume is obligatory. Most of the Pueblos used to make their own but none of them weave now. They come to Hopi bringing turquoise to trade in the ancient manner.

Now that men no longer make stone tools or bows and arrows, their other arts all have to do with ceremony and are not revealed to a boy until after his second initiation. This is the great, the solemn

40

event of the Hopi year. It takes place in November after the harvest is in and every Hopi, no matter how far afield he may be, is expected home. White people are asked to leave the mesa; women and the uninitiated stay inside the houses; a line of cornmeal is drawn across the path that leads to the village and Zuni, Navajo, even Hopi from the other mesas, respect it and stay away.

We shall not pry into secrets so religiously kept, but all may know that this is the time when a growing youth is "made a Hopi". He joins one of four secret societies who, on these nights, go dancing and singing through the village, masked and costumed. After that he may take part in the regular rain dances. In fact for the first year, he *must* take part, for dancing with the Hopi is a religious duty. Initiation used to take place at fourteen but, since at that age Hopi boys have usually been at boarding school, it is now put off to eighteen or even later. Every Hopi has a right to it, even though he be disloyal or insane. A candidate has even been bailed out of jail for this very purpose.

After initiation comes manhood and responsibilities among the first of which is marriage. Hopi youths do not have a choice of brides, at least theoretically. In olden times it was the maiden who, coached perhaps by her mother, chose. She had been brought up of course to realize that all the men in her own clan were brothers, even though not really related and her thoughts would never stray toward them. On the village rabbit hunt she might have seen some active youth and to him she would carry a plate of corn cake. If he was willing he had only eat the cake without a word of proposal.

41

He would now go to the girl's family to live, for such is the Hopi way. First there would be a series of gifts and return gifts, ceremonies and return ceremonies, almost like a dance in its complications, but with a purpose much more practical. This wedding, like those of the European aristocracy, is really an alliance between the families of the bride and groom, who will have duties toward each other forever after. Naturally each family wants to know if the other can be depended on for gifts of cornmeal and help in ceremonies at the proper times, so they try each other out. First the girl goes to the boy's house and grinds corn for four whole days so that his family will know that she is industrious. Then his relatives—men of course—must collect cotton and weave her a wedding outfit. Its items are prescribed as sternly as white satin and orange blossoms used to be for the Whites and like these, they are falling into disuse.

Once every girl expected: one white cotton blanket with tasselled corners which was to be folded around her as a dress; one large white blanket with red border; one sash and a little wicker roll to tie them in. She got a pair of moccasins too, beautiful long ones, made of a whole white buckskin to fit her tiny feet and topped by thick puttees which made them look even smaller. Those moccasins must be a concession to a change of style that took place long ago for they take more buckskin than ever came the way of the old sandal-wearing Hopi. The custom of the bridal robe is very old and even though the bride will hardly ever wear it again, she must have it when she dies to bear her over the edge of the Grand Canyon, as the groom's basket plaque bears him.

All the time the men are weaving the girl cooks for them so they have a good chance to judge of their new relative-in-law. At last they escort her with her new possessions triumphantly home to her mother, but even yet the husband does not join her. She has to grind more cornmeal to "pay for" him and that is where the basket tray comes in. Some of those customs have lapsed nowadays, but few of the Hopi are reconciled. One wedding which took place with a mere license and some words from a justice of the peace, is regarded quite like a trial marriage. It wasn't "paid for".

The young people are adult Hopi now and they must practise the hospitality, modesty and neighborliness which are the duties of all good citizens. Though they may furnish the house with oilcloth, chairs and canned goods, their minds will be furnished with a belief in the ancient religion, a following of old ideals that they do not fully realize. Common sense tells them to buy the canned goods when they are available, but it does not tell them to slip out of harmony with the powers of rain and fertility. Nor does it tell them to relinquish loyalty to a democratic organization older than any their white neighbors have made.

Yet the Whites often wonder what the Hopi system of government is. There seems no executive empowered to act for a town. No police! No laws! And such leaders as there are appear to be now priests, now family heads. There is in fact a minimum of organization and such, one imagines, must have been the case with the ancient seed gatherers who first began to farm. Yet Hopi arrangements are clear and workable, even though they are to a modern written constitution as a small growing plant is to a well-planned machine.

43

There is, in the first place, no Hopi nation. Each village acts entirely for itself—with that one exception when they threw out the Spaniards. Their bond is one of tradition and language and even these change noticeably from mesa to mesa. Within the village, government is not noticeable. No officers who could actually be called executives. (That was a trial to the Spaniards. They simply could not find anyone to be responsible for agreements). No police. No penalties. The group of leaders who meet when anything is to be decided answer better to our idea of priests or family heads than to that of a town council. Priests and family heads they are and usually both at once. The drive which governs all Hopi acts and keeps the people together, like a flock of flying birds which seem to have no leader, is religion and family.

The first thing a Hopi child must learn if he is to know how to behave, is the clan he belongs to. A clan in this case is not like the Scotch ones, famous in history, which consisted say, of Roderick Dhu and all descendants whose fathers bore the famous name of Dhu. Hopi count their descent through the female ancestor and a child belongs to his mother's clan, not to his father's. Matriarchy? The *rule of women? Not in the least. Just a convenient way of counting descent* for the place of a Hopi woman is very much in the home and the head of the clan is a man. But he is not her husband; he is her brother, descended from the same mother, belonging to the same clan. He it is who conducts clan ceremonies and takes charge of clan affairs. He is the family head. Say he belongs to the Bear clan. He may marry a woman from Tansy Mustard and then his children will

44

. . . .at the base of the mesa you may note a spring with a sprig of evergreen planted by its brink. . . .

....and naked children find their one real bathtub....

....now he may have clothes from the mail order house.... ——

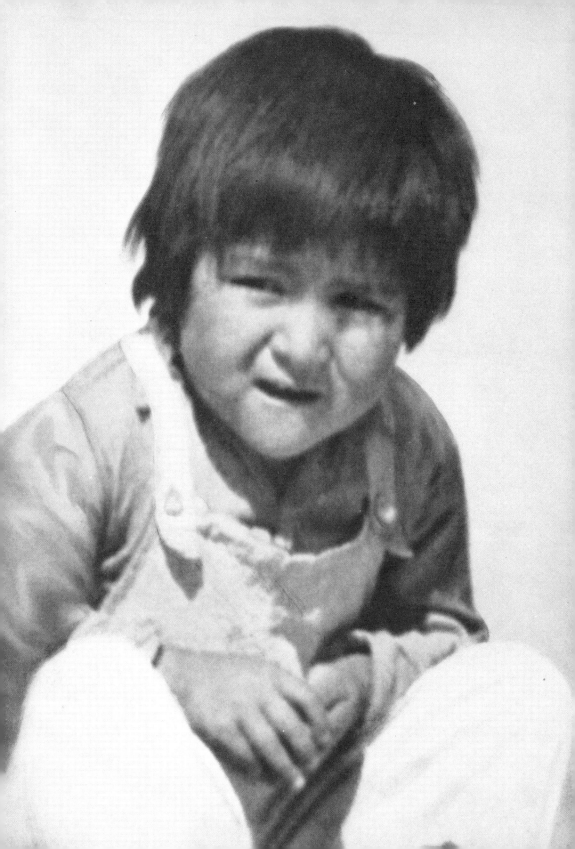

be Tansy Mustard people like their mother. He cannot pass his clan responsibilities on to them. His heirs must be his sister's children who are Bears.

Inheritance with the Hopi goes down in a peculiar zigzag; uncle to nephew, and it brings strange corollaries. The houses of the Hopi belong to women and a man when he marries goes out to his new home as a bride used to among the Whites. The sacred things of his own clan remain in the house of his sister and he goes back there for ceremonies. If he and his wife separate, he will go back there to live, as a white woman returns to her father. It used to puzzle white reformers at first, when they found that if a child was a problem case, it was his uncle rather than his father who should be asked to deal with him. It bothered them even more to find that a widow had no right to her dead husband's property. It belonged to his nephew of course, and she would inherit from her own family. Then the white people began to wonder what had happened to fatherly affection and they found that it went on just the same as elsewhere. Hopi fathers were not heads of families in our sense and yet the family was affectionate and united exactly like any other.

The Hopi have about thirty of these mother clans with members from most of them in each village. The tale goes that, after the famous emergence from underground, the clans all wandered separately until one by one, they got to the mesas. The first clan to found a village took charge of the land and its head man was head of the village. As other clans arrived, he questioned each one, "Will you be

45

← ....when Hopi children play....

useful to us? Have you good magic?" The newcomers proved they could bring the rain or make the corn grow and the First Families let them in and gave them land. They did not give it to individuals however. Rugged individualism was unheard of in those days and the land went to the clan as a whole. So it is owned today and each clan chief is supposed to distribute it among the members as he sees fit.

This would have been a dangerous situation if the clan chief had not been an honorable man, but he was that and more, he was a priest. Every clan had brought up from underground the sacred things that made its magic and these the clan chief kept for them, passing them on to the wisest of his sister's sons. They had also their sacred ceremony which had gained them admission and this they conducted once a year for the benefit of the village. The clan chief was the priest and the clan members his assisstants and they had a sacred kiva called by the clan name, so really clan head and priest were one. Every Hopi had his clan family which was in effect his church and his family head who was his priest. To be a good man meant to help the clan members and never to get any of them into trouble. This meant being self-supporting, so as not to use up clan resources. It meant not committing misdemeanors because then other people would blame the clan and the clan would have to pay. In fact it covered everything. And if any Hopi was not a good man, there was only one penalty: the clan would dislike him. It does not sound like much of a punishment but to the old Hopi, it was like being put out of the only job he knew and for which he had trained all his life. Modern reformers who urge a Hopi child; "Come! Come! You

46

mustn't mind what people say," little know what powerful, age-old machinery they are combatting.

We have now some key to the Hopi ceremonies. There is one for almost every month in the year and with their costumes, dances and processions they furnish, says one traveler, "the best round of free entertainment in the world". But these masks and dramas are not provided for entertainment. They are the ceremonies brought by the different clans as their passport to Hopiland and they are spread through the year as continouus magic for rain and increase. The flute ceremony was brought by the Flute clan, the snake dance by the Snake clan. We must pause to admit that the arrangement is no longer quite so simple. Ceremonies have been lost, leaders have changed, and those who want the straight of the situation will have to go a little further into detail.

One of the old men of a clan is indeed the head priest of a ceremony which he hands down in the clan and which is often held in the clan kiva, but not only by clan members. Others have been allowed to join, generally because they were sick and wanted to be helped by the magic ceremony. Now there is a Snake clan and a snake society, a Flute clan and a flute society. No one is born a member of one of these societies as he used to be born a member of the clan. Clan members and non-members join voluntarily. Anyone could be a Snake priest by request of himself or his parents, or the Snakes might even invite him.

These societies and the clans are the ruling powers in the Hopi villages and their heads are the council. Over them all is the Town

47

Chief, the head of the first clan to arrive, but he is no commanding executive. The council discusses everything and, unless it agrees unanimously, there can be no action at all. White men have despaired about that, for there is no way to push through a Hopi vote and get quick action, and on the other hand, there is no way to get dictatorship in a Hopi town. Their democracy is as complete as any on earth.

The government by family heads and priests actually *is* the religion. The ceremonies are performed to grow the crops and to keep the people alive and a good citizen participates in them as in modern cities he would serve on committees. Of a good Hopi it is said: "He is a quiet man. You never hear of him. And he is in all the dances." To describe those dances would need volumes and such volumes have already been published, but we can give a brief summary of what constitutes a religious ceremony to the Hopi.

To begin with it has two versions: a long one, for the people on earth; and a short one, six months later for the people in the underworld. Down there winter is summer and night is day, so if the priests on earth have celebrated in August they know that in March their brethren in the underworld will be doing the same and they celebrate a little in sympathy. The ceremony on earth which is our concern is really nine days long, or at least five, though the public sees only one. The other days are taken up in preparation, inviting the gods, and honoring their altar.

First the priests have the coming ceremony announced by the village crier. Then *they meet in the kiva* and begin their preparations of bringing wood and preparing costumes. White men would not call this prosaic work a part of the ceremony but to the Hopi it is all sacred and to be done under sacred conditions. They prepare offerings to the gods which are usually feathers, tied intricately to sticks, or to handmade cotton string. The whole Southwest regards feathers as an offering. The Hopi have made of them a system of heraldry by which every supernatural being has his feathers and size of stick and methods of tying. Some young man from the society is sent out in kilt, handwoven after the ancient manner, to carry the invitations to the gods in spring or mountain shrine. The priests set up the altar on the floor of the kiva. They are elaborate works of art, the altars. Perhaps there is a design on the floor in colored sand (the Navajo are not the only ones to make sandpaintings and the pueblo people may have taught them). Upon it is a bowl of water expressing the endless wish for rain. Around it may stand corn ears, or sticks that mean corn, or there may be beans, or squash or cotton clouds, or sunflowers, or images of the gods. It it a dramatic representation of the power of the supernaturals and the wishes of man.

Sitting about it the priests blow tobacco smoke as incense to the six directions for above and below count as directions among most pueblo people as well as the points of the compass. With each cloud of smoke they sing songs of corn and growth, like this one which belongs to Powamu, the feast of early bean planting.

(To the north)

Ha-o, my mother
Ha-o, my mother
Due north, yellow corn ear, my mother

49

Due southward, blooming corn plant
Decorate our faces
Bless us with flowers
Thus being face-decorated
Being blessed with flowers
We shall be delighted
We shall be delighted.
Ha-o, my mother.

(To the west)

Ha-o my mother
Ha-o my mother
Due west, blue corn ear, my mother
Due eastward, blooming bluebird flower
Decorate our faces
Bless us with flowers
Thus being face-decorated
Being blessed with flowers
We shall be delighted
We shall be delighted.
Ha-o my mother.

(To the south)

Ha-o my mother
Ha-o my mother
Due south, red corn ear, my mother
Due northward, blooming maiden blossom
Decorate our faces
Bless us with flowers.
Thus, being face-decorated
Being blessed with flowers,
We shall be delighted
We shall be delighted.
Ha-o my mother.

(To the east)
Ha-o my mother
Ha-o my mother.
Due east, white corn ear, my mother
Due westward, blooming butterfly flower
Decorate our faces
Bless us with flowers.
Thus, being face-decorated,
Being blessed with flowers,
We shall be delighted,
We shall be delighted.
Ha-o my mother
   (To the northeast which stands for above)
Ha-o my mother.
Due above, black corn ear, my mother.
Due downward, blooming sunflower,
Decorate our faces.
Bless us with flowers.
Thus, being face-decorated,
Being blessed with flowers,
We shall be delighted.
We shall be delighted.
Ha-o my mother.
   (To the southwest, which stands for below).
Ha-o my mother,
Ha-o my mother.
Due below, sweet corn ear, my mother.
Due upward, blooming, all kinds of flowers.
Decorate our faces.
Bless us with flowers.
Thus, being face-decorated,
Being blessed with flowers,
We shall be delighted.
We shall be delighted.
Ha-o, my mother.

51

In the second four days of the nine-day vigil, the gods arrive. Generally they are represented by priests, masked and costumed for a dance or a primitive miracle play. It is here that Hopi men have their chance for artistry. None of the paraphernalia may be made by women, and men spend weeks, even months all told, in deft and beautiful work on costumes, prayersticks and stage setting. Besides artistry, they show mechanical invention. The painted collapsible frame which is pulled in and out to represent lightning, the great serpents which swing their gourd heads on necks of painted cotton— these contrivances astonish the Whites who see them, but they are distinctly Indian, made of ancient materials and used perhaps for centuries.

For the ceremony to which the Whites come oftenest, the Snake Dance, no contrivances are necessary. Nor is anyone needed to represent the gods, for they are present in person in the form of snakes invited to dance with their younger brothers, the priests of the Snake society. The Snake clan, says the story, were once reptiles and they traveled in a buckskin bag hung at the end of a rainbow. Where the bag dropped to earth they made their home and took on human bodies, but they had no magic until, says another myth, one of their young men, wandering to the land of the snakes, learned their ceremonies and brought home a snake maiden as a bride. It was at the direction of the Snake people, their elder brothers, that the clan members every summer before the rainy season went out to the four points of the compass, captured all the snakes they could and brought them to the kiva so that they might take back to the

52

It takes hours to grind first on the coarse slab.... ⟶

supernaturals a prayer for rain. They do this now. For the first four days of the ceremony the Snake priests seek their brothers, east, north, west and south. For the second four they honor them by prayers and washing. The Hopi wash their own black hair in yucca suds before every ceremony, but since the snakes cannot do this, their younger brothers bathe them.

On the last day the snakes dance in public just as all gods dance in Hopi ceremonies. Each "elder brother" is carried in the mouth of a Hopi priest while another priest behind him strokes gently with feathers on a stick handle to keep him quiet and content. After a round of the plaza the "elder brother" is set free and a third priest gathers him up to await the end of the ceremony. Before he is picked up, there may be some screaming and scurrying among white spectators and it is not impossible that the gatherer indulges his sense of drama. Certain it is that the priests often let their "elder brothers" go much further than a white priest might consider safe. Before the ceremony is over each gatherer is holding a handful of snakes and the members of the Antelope society who have been acting as a chorus shake their rattles with one hand and hold the extra snakes in the other. After every snake has danced, all are thrown on a circle of cornmeal in the center of the plaza. Cornmeal is supposed to be sufficient to keep them in bounds, although white spectators do not understand that. The priests pick up the snakes by handfuls and run with them again to the four points of the compass, whence they will bear to the supernaturals the message that the Hopi ask for rain. The priests take an emetic to vomit away the danger caused by such close contact

53

If she lives on First Mesa she will make pottery....

with magic power. Do they also take an antidote for snakebite? No white man has ever found proof of it and the chemist who studied the Snake Dance reported only that the snakes might have been weary from handling and might have temporarily exhausted their venom. Those Whites who consider that a snake is everywhere the symbol for evil might be interested to note that with the Hopi the snake, which lives in wet places, is a symbol for rain and life.

When the patrons of other societies dance in the plaza, they dance in the shape of men or women with flowing hair, wearing the old Hopi costume of embroidered kilt or blanket dress. Most beloved and frequent of these vistants are the kachinas who come from San Francisco Peaks, the home of the clouds. They arrive in March, when the early beans are planted, and stay until August, when the rainy season begins and when all the Hopi gather to bid them farewell. For the intervening months they are hovering near the towns and on many an afternoon the sound of their male singing floats from the plazas. In these days when Hopi men have wage work, kachinas seem to come on Saturday afternoons. You may see in the sunlight a line of kilted figures prancing with military precision to the rhythm of their shaking rattles. They wear masks of white, yellow, or copper blue which stare unmoved over a ruff of spruce, the symbol of undying growth. *The Hopi men make dolls to represent these kachinas*, whose name is legion, and give them to their children at the feast of the bean planting which is their Christmas. Beautifully colored, deftly made, the white person may find them grotesque, but those distorted features are the means the Hopi has taken for representing something completely unearthy, non-human.

Do they believe in these beings as their ancestors did? It would be hard for the Hopi, as for a member of any church, to say how much of his creed has distilled into poetry. The Hopi are loyal to a way of life, and perhaps increasingly loyal as a choice of other ways is spread before them. There is hope in the deliberation with which they approach that choice. American life may show new possibilities when expressed through Hopi tenacity, craftsmanship, and invincible democracy.

3

Zuni the Center

The Zuni say that, when the disc of earth was new and quivering, they wandered over its surface until they found the center. There they settled down. From the point of view of many a student they are right. Other Indians tell this tale of the center, but the Zuni, psychologically if not geographically, seem at the center of the old pueblo world. There, can be found in the highest degree that group spirit which marked the old farming communities. There, the great dance dramas mark the seasons with a pageantry as splendid as that of a city opera stage.

In these days Zuni lies near the edge of pueblo country. Spanish travelers used to pass through this rock-rimmed valley where the little stream shines among the cornfields and still find themselves many desert leagues away from the Rio Grande and civilization. For the most part they left Zuni out of their calculations just as they did Hopi. Neither had a grant of land, for the whole desert was left to them undisputed, except of course by wild Navajo and Apache. Neither paid taxes. Neither therefore, had to suppress its old customs which hold in great part to this day. The two neighbors are age-long intimates who must have been exchanging knowledge for centuries, and we think of them together, at least as compared with the other Pueblos.

Yet they are not close relatives, as far as language shows. The Zuni language, spoken only in one narrow valley, was thought for a long time to have no relatives in North America. Zuni customs pointed strongly to Mexico where corn grew in the early days of New World history, where priests watched for the solstices, and where the ceremonies swung through the year with the same gorgeous regularity which they have at Zuni. Now some think the language has yielded a faint resemblance to the huge family of Mexican and northern languages which includes the Hopi. Resemblances not always so faint turn up in the other pueblos, but the Zuni resemblance is faint indeed. This little handful of farmers must have separated ages ago from any others who spoke their tongue. There is no indication as to when it was or which way they traveled, but there is no doubt that they have lived in houses and worn clothes for centuries. The houses indeed may have dirt floors and lack running water, but in poetry, in pageantry, in craftmanship, even in daily living, the Zuni have the touch of those long used to the arts. If they brought these from another civilization, thay do not remember it. They are as well established in their

58

rock-rimmed valley as though they had come there direct from underground.

They say that they did. They say it was the Sun Father himself who called them out from the fourth womb of earth to keep him company.

"Yes indeed. In this world there was no one at all. Always the sun came up. Always he went in. No one in the morning gave him sacred meal; no one gave him prayersticks; it was very lonely. He said to his two children: 'You will go into the fourth womb. Your father your mothers...' — and he named all the priests who still conduct the Zuni ceremonies — 'you will bring them out yonder into the light of your sun father'."

The youths shot arrows into earth's dark womb and entered. They kindled fire, the first the underground people had ever seen, and they heard a voice beside them.

"Ouch! What have you there?" he said. He fell down crouching. He had a slimy horn, a slimy tail, he was slimy all over, with webbed hands. The elder brother said: "Poor thing. Put out the light."

There is a touch of evolution about this story, for the slimy Underground People were not really human at first, but the Sun Children cut off their tails and slashed their webbed hands and feet making them dry in the process. That was not until they had led them up from Earth's fourth womb, climbing by a pine, a spruce, a pinyon, and a cottonwood. At every pause they sang all their sacred songs, which are the very ones that are sung now when the dancers stamp in the plaza, waving spruce boughs and rattles, and masked in turquoise and yellow and white. Thus they came up through sulphur-smell-inside-the-world, soot-inside-the world, fog-inside-the-world, until they "stood forth into the daylight of their Sun Father".

Then they went seaching for the Earth Center. They were wild

59

people then, eating grass seed "like the birds on the mesas". They met the Dew People who had with them the six beautiful Corn Maidens, carrying corn, colored for the six directions. It was the same which the Zuni raise now: yellow for north, blue for west, red for south, white for east, vari-colored for above, and black for below. Is this an echo of the farmer-immigrants who brought corn to the Southwest?

They camped with the Dew People and with them they built their towns. By dint of sending runners to the edge of the earth-disc in both directions they finally located its center and built a town there with five others around it. The center town is still there. From the windows of its stone houses comes the hum of sewing machines. Mixed with the sound of rattles from the plaza is the clank of the automobile. When the evening sun fades from the red cliffs where the Zuni used to flee for refuge, there shines out above the hidden shrines an airplane beacon, but Zuni ancient or modern, is still the center for that gracious artistry of the Pueblos, the ceremony which is government and the government which is ceremony.

Earth Center has moved a little since the Spaniards first found it, and it has shrunk. In 1540 there were six small towns spread through a pleasant valley with Halona the center, almost where Zuni is now. Here was no mountain fortress like those in which the Hopi held out against their enemies. The villagers, when they had to, fled to their sacred mountain, Towalayane, and sometimes stayed aloft for years, but they always came back to the terraced houses among the cornfields. Each village held two hundred people or more, so the chronic-

The hardest part of the tray is to get it started . . . .

The mother will have a bee at which many of her friends make centers.

When you buy one of these products of Hopi craft, a waste basket for example, —
you will know it comes from Third Mesa.

lers say, in the houses banked up four and five storeys high. Within their dark rooms joined by small, high doors, through which one squeezed as through a window, women knelt grinding the vari-colored corn, as they do now. They were dressed as now in dark robes of homespun cotton. Here and there an old man squatted before a loom. Other men prodded the fields with a digging stick and down to the river came maidens with their water jars painted in white and black and red.

Such were the Zuni villages, but far different was the picture of them which formed in Spanish minds. When rumors of "large and powerful villages to the north" penetrated down through the mountains to Mexico, the treasure of the Aztecs had long ago been thrown into the melting pot. Those who had missed their share of it were straining and jumping for another chance, and almost out of thin air they concocted the myth of the Seven Cities of Cibola.

Our Southwest at that time was a wild northern desert where almost anything might exist, even a water route to the Atlantic. If there were cities there of course they would be seven, for seven was a magic number. And of course they would have gold. The Zuni, who had never worked metal in their lives, were reported to have vessels and sweat scrapers of gold, while the doorsills of their houses were inlaid with turquoise. Every disgruntled adventurer in New Spain began to yearn for the Seven Cities and the only question was where, in the thousands of square miles to the north, they could be found. A negro slave discovered them.

The adventures of that negro are among the most grotesque and fantastic in all history. His name was Estéban and he got shipwrecked

61

←— .... rule of women? Not in the least. Just a convenient way of counting descent.

with three Spaniards somewhere on the Gulf of Mexico. Thence they set out to walk to Mexico City. Naked and starving, the three white bodies and one black dragged themselves through Texas, Chihuahua, Sonora and no one knows whereelse while, Indians who are now extinct acclaimed them as gods. None of them was ever the same man again and especially not Estéban who had been a slave. After years of incredible exploits he arrived again among "the Christians" as the Spaniards always called themselves—and he was a slave again.

He listened in the background while his companions recounted their adventures, among them tall tales of tall cities in the northern desert. There was nothing about gold, but the imagination of their hearers supplied that. Everyone wanted to be taken north after it, but the three white men were tired and ready for civilization. Estéban was not. Eagerly he agreed to lead any one to the north, even to the Seven Cities, so the governor himself sent out a party with Estéban as guide. The first Spanish subject to enter the Southwest was a negro.

The rest of the party consisted of a learned priest and a few soldiers. The priest went slowly, preaching on the way and securing subjects for the king of Spain. Estéban went scouting ahead and, since he could neither read nor write, he and the priest arranged a system of signals. If all went well and it was safe for Fray Marcos to follow, what more appropriate than to send a cross? He was to send a little cross if he found anything of medium importance; a bigger one if it was very important; and, "if it were more important than New Spain" (which was all of Mexico), he was to send a large cross.

Estéban disappeared into the wilds and crosses kept coming. The first was as big as a man, the second the same. The excited friar sent messages to wait, but all he got was another cross. He reached what is now the Mexican border. He went north into the No Man's Land which is now our Southwest. Or did he? Many a Spaniard and many a modern student has doubted his tale, but all believe that the negro Estéban got to the first Zuni town and disappeared forever.

He had been a lord for a short time, the commander of an invading party like the mailed Spaniards who had been his masters. The chroniclers say he decked his black body with rattles and feathers as he marched through the Indian settlements collecting turquoise and women. Trains of adoring Indians followed him, carrying the gifts presented to him and "believing that, under his protection, they could traverse the whole world without any danger". No wonder he did not want the friar to catch up with him.

Like a great lord and medicine man he strutted up to Hawikuh, the first Zuni town, demanding his turquoise and women. "But it seemed unreasonable," said the Zuni afterward, "to say that the people in the country from which he came were white and that he was sent by them, he being black". Moreover they say he killed and assaulted women which "the Christians" never did. The Zuni killed him. Some say they cut up his body and sent pieces of it to all the pueblos and some say they kept his bones as a proof that the strange new creatures who were invading their country were mortal and could die. They sent word to their sister villages to kill any new ones without fear "and if they did not dare do this, they should send word so those of Cibola could come and do it".

63

But "those of Cibola" did not know what they were undertaking. One year they enjoyed their triumph and then Coronado marched through the Southwest straight to Hawikuh. The Zuni fought him. They were not like the Hopi who could practice passive resistance while two hundred miles of desert protected their smiling evasions. Their little Hawikuh was the very goal of the invading army, and that army was hungry. "We could not obtain anything to eat," reported one of the soldiers, "unless we captured it. . . . . . So it was necessary to attack and kill some of them."

It was a pathetic battle. The Zuni threw stones from their walls at the glittering helmet of Coronado and hurt him so that his face was sore afterward. Four or five Spaniards had arrow wounds and some horses were killed. Then the Indians moved out of their town and took refuge on the sacred mountain whither they must flee from time to time through the three centuries to come. The hungry Spaniards moved in.

They found one of the ancient, terraced towns, four-, five-, and six-storeys high, say the chroniclers, stocked with maize, beans, and squashes enough to last the winter. They consumed these while the Zuni shivered and starved on their holy mountain, and they renamed the town Granada. That town is in ruins now as are the five others which the Spaniards visited and called by high sounding European names long forgotten. There was no gold in any of them, and eventually the brass helmets went glittering away over the plains and the Zuni came home.

For the next hundred years the Zuni came out to meet visiting

Christians with presents of food even before they were asked. It paid them well. They were not so far as the Hopi from the brass hats of New Spain and occasionally some new official decided to show his zeal by venturing out through the desert to look them over. Though the Zuni showed themselves "most domestic, obedient and loyal", the visitor, as a rule, turned round immediately and hastened toward civilization, leaving the record of his exploit carved on the smooth flanks of Inscription Rock.

This tall mesa stands at the south entrance of the Zuni valley, just where the expeditions would pass it as they came and went. Camped by the pool of milky, alkaline water that drips from its sides, the leaders dug out, with dagger points, their ornamental inscriptions in strangely spelled old Spanish—or more likely they had it done by someone who could spell a little. "Here passed" Oñate, the first governor of New Mexico, and De Vargas who pacified it after the rebellion; also Governor Silva de Nieto "whose indubitable arm and valor has overcome the impossible... That he may well pass to Zuni and carry the faith". It was only a few years after this inscription about the faith that the Zuni killed two padres.

Nevertheless padres came in the end. The first gentle Franciscan succeeded in baptising a whole village, but that did not last. The next two received the crown of martyrdom. Ultimately however, the faith was carried and Zuni was subdued. "As they themselves had desired and wished," says one of the inscriptions. A geographic accident prevented their maintaining the wild independence of Hopi. They were not far enough away and they were not on a mesa. Inward

65

independence was quite another matter. Zuni raised wheat and sheep and went to church, and Zuni maintained its individuality so completely that it is even today the focus of pueblo life: the earth center.

The rebellion came in 1680 and the Zuni joined it. Tradition says that they even swung the Hopi into line, for before this the Peaceful had prevented disturbance because they preferred their own quiet methods. Tradition says also that there was one Zuni priest who was not killed. True, he disappeared, but there are lasting tales that, since he was a good man of whom they were really fond, the Zuni offered to spare his life if he would dress like them and be adopted into the tribe. He accepted. The Zuni moved out of all their towns as they did when danger threatened and took refuge on holy Towayalane. Perhaps the priest was with them and perhaps he saved the holy images and the church vessels. At least when the Spaniards came back twelve years later, they found the people still on the mountain but preserving those sacred things which "rejoiced the conquerors as evidence of their earlier Christian state".

The Spaniards' return marks the beginning of modern Zuni. Wild Apache had destroyed one of their villages. The inhabitants of all five others had huddled for twelve years on their nearby mountain afraid to come down and meet the punishment awaiting them. When a sadder and wiser Spain offered peace, few went back to the old homes. They gathered in Halona, the Earth Center, which grew until it sheltered them all, with four new villages among the fields for summer residence. They appointed a secular governor as Spanish decree demanded, and he is still there to perform the extraneous business of dealing with the Whites. They built a church. Let no one think however, that the art, the ceremonies, or the life of Zuni has paled. The priests of the sun and the rain still meet to rule the village. Kilted men, with long hair flowing, run every month to some shrine in the hills to plant offerings to the supernaturals. All through the year the plaza echoes to the stamp and rattle of dancing worshippers. The church is in ruins.

Zuni went through some bad years while Spain declined and the new republic of Mexico struggled hopelessly with wild Navajo and Apache. No one helped the little pueblo in her own struggles and she did what she could. At one time the Zuni had acquired a hundred Navajo captives and feeding them grew expensive, so they put them in the plaza, with two Zuni warriors at each corner, and told them to escape if they could. None did.

In 1848 Mexico was rather forcibly persuaded to give up a large stretch of her northern country to the United States which wished to build a railroad. The country included Zuni. In 1877 a reservation was set aside for these "honest and virtuous people" who were such a relief after the turbulent nomads. It took a long time for the declining population to take an upward turn, but by 1933 it was 2021, with an increase of 82 since 1910. The four outside farming villages, which had been only camps, began to grow now that danger was over. If they and the population go on increasing, there may some day actually be seven cities of Cibola.

There are day schools at two of them already and a high school at Zuni proper. Every child in Zuni speaks English now and no one

67

stays out of school, say the reports, any more than in a white community. A few miles from the town stand a hospital and a sub-agency, and there are two churches, a Catholic and a Protestant, to replace the ruined one. That one the Zuni will neither repair nor destroy. "For it is the missa house of our fathers who are dead, and dead is the missa house. May the fathers be made to live again by adding of meat to their bones? How then may the missa house be made alive again by the adding of mud to its walls?"

The church may be dead but Zuni is alive. You may approach it from Gallup, that modern town with main streets named after its two progenitors, Railroad and Coal; but if you would gain some of the thrill felt by early Spaniards, approach it from the south, past Inscription Rock. On an August day the yellow sunflowers and lavender beebalm make a foreground of sunset colors for the red crags of Towayalane. *The fields by the river glow a brillant green.* The Spaniards used to march two days from the Rock to Halona, but we cover the distance in an hour along a road punctuated with automobile signs, "SLOW". We enter a village which is part Halona and part the modern Zuni.

We *drive through modern streets among houses* which are *no longer terraced.* They are still made of red stone but the ladders are gone and instead appear doors and windows, their frames gleaming with white paint and screened. Around some of them are gardens of morning glories and sweet peas, a sure sign of civilization, for Indians uninfluenced never took time to raise flowers. Above the town rises a water tower, backed by an ultra modern school, all glass and cut stone and well tended gardens.

....they meet in the kiva....

The fields by the river glow a brilliant green....

— *The Hopi men make dolls to represent these kachinas...*

. . . . drive through modern streets among houses . . . . no longer terraced.

It looks almost like a suburb in Spanish style, or perhaps a hilly village of Mexico; but here is none of the dramatic idleness which northerners associate with the land of mañana. Within the clean, whitewashed rooms women are moving busily from kitchen cabinet to oilcloth-covered table. The men are in the fields at wheat threshing, at the store, or the gas station. *Through a window a man* and wife *may be seen bending over the delicate* turquoise *jewelry* which they sell for white man's money. The most original of these, like Ike, are Navajo, ancient enemies, who now live peacefully intermarried in their midst. Maidens patter through the streets, but some of them are 4H Club girls, coming from a lesson in canning tomatoes. *Others carry water jars on their heads as of old*, but they are going not to the ancient well, but to one of the eighteen hydrants which bring water from the water tower. Nevertheless in inner rooms, since this is summer, there are priests reciting the ancient words which will bring rain to the Zuni, the Navajo, the Whites and the whole world.

The Zuni do not seem bewildered by these changes, for they have the interest they have always had: crops. The colored corn, named for the six directions, has been not only a means of livelihood but a religion. It still is. Ground cornmeal is the Zuni sacrifice; a perfect corn ear is the badge of membership in a medicine society; corn ears lie beside the babies to protect them; and corn is still the staple food. Though the Zuni often fast for religious purposes, they never fast from corn which is life itself.

They raise it in the same way that they always did. Their little fields lie near the river so that water can be dammed in around every

69

cherished plant. The Zuni used to carry water to these fields in dry weather. Recently the government has managed a river dam for them and a strip of irrigated land. They accepted the innovation, but they used the new land for wheat and alfalfa. For corn, their system of prayers and hard work was already complete.

They had no objection to learning to farm for money and luxuries. *Near the houses are* the so-called *"waffle-gardens"*, arranged so that each plant of chili can have its own supply of water, and not a drop is wasted. Artists and craftsmen as they were, the Zuni were quite open to new ideas. Out in the country you may see their neat stone farm houses with shining white-curtained windows. A man in blue jeans and cowboy hat may be following the plow while his wife, in ancient dress and gaily flowered shawl, goes out to feed the chickens. When the waving wheat is ripe, they rent a thresher. There are two, one belonging to the government, one to a Zuni, but if they are in a hurry they do as the Spanish padres taught them—*drive* six or eight *horses round and round* on a circular earthen floor *till their hoofs have pounded out the grains.*

"It's hard work," admitted a farmer whom I watched, as he mopped his brow with the sleeve of a purple silk shirt; but he was like other Zuni, not afraid of hard work. Neither was his wife who stood ready to sift the chaff from the wheat grains just as the Zuni did centuries ago, perhaps even when they ate grass seed "like birds on the mesas". She took a huge flat basket full of grains and chaff and jogged it up and down in the wind. The chaff bounced to the top, the heavy wheat to the bottom and then, with a little sidewise jerk, the chaff was tipped overboard.

70

"Now will you grind it on the old grinding stone?" I asked her. Of course not. The government has a mill and the Zuni are quite willing to pay machine driven stones to do what the women used to do with two small stones and back muscle.

Almost like a white farmer, you may think; but follow the Zuni home. His crops, like the Hopi crops, belong to the woman of the family, and so does the house. Unless this is a very modern man indeed he has come to live with his wife in the residence of her family. There she spends her life beside her mother and her married sisters, their one room dwellings, plastered by their own hands, crammed side by side like cells in a beehive. Thither come their husbands, some for life, some till divorce. They bring their harvest home to the women who use it as they see fit. Until recently no Zuni man quarrelled with this arrangement. His own interest and his honor he got from ceremony; and his principle was: let the woman take charge of our material goods, let the man be occupied with the gods who provide them.

Many a woman of the modern world might have liked to watch this principle work out, but it is changing. No one rebelled against the old system. No one even realized that it was threatened. Then the Zuni got more sheep. Long ago the missionaries gave them a few and these were taken over by the men which was natural since the men were the family hunters and they simply contributed a sheep to the family feast instead of going out after deer. Little by little they got so many sheep that not all were killed. Now they have enough to sell the wool and receive money. There is a rule that crops should

71

be given to the women, but no rule about money, which they keep. Thus civilization has delivered a backhand blow at the old Zuni system. As long as the Zuni pursued their old ways the men seemed satisfied with the women in control of funds. Now there is some dissatisfaction in families when a man becomes independent.

With the new ways life is perhaps less hard. A woman can have several dresses now instead of the single, handwoven one which used to last a lifetime. She can send to the mail order house for stockings and shoes instead of waiting for the men to get a buckskin and make her an elaborate pair of white moccasins. Of course shoes make her feet look large whereas the huge tubular moccasins kept them almost invisible. She is freed now from the back-breaking labor of grinding corn and from the pottery making which used to consume all her leisure time in simply keeping the family supplied with utensils. *If she makes pots now she makes them for sale.*

The Zuni jar was never outstanding for thinness and texture and it is not water-tight at all, but there is a lovable individuality about its bulging shape, with the orange bottom and the stiff legged deer, in his "house" of flowers, the red "breath line" running to his heart. That pot represents all the old Zuni art that is left except the secret fabrications made for ceremonies. Men no longer weave, but trade with the shrewd and pertinacious Hopi for their ceremonial dress. Zuni men and women have become adept at silver work and in mounting turquoise. But, as in other activities, they tend to conservatism in pattern, and their jewelry, although delicate and well-executed, is

72

monotonous. Navajo silversmiths have moved into Zuni and have taken over the original work in silver, for the Zuni do not cut new dies and hence keep on with their particular style.

Recently a new and amusing art has developed—like silver work, one which brings in cash. You may see whole families chattering gayly over the sewing of colored beads, which was never a Zuni craft. No Indians used glass beads before the coming of the Whites, but white people think Indians ought to do beadwork. *Somehow the art of sewing beads* around a lucky rabbit's foot *got started*, gained impetus, and now has become an indispensable economic factor in this pueblo. It has so developed that now tiny dolls are beaded and these are not only amusing but they have the value of caricature. The Zuni woman has her short skirt, woven belt, and wound legging depicted in beads; *the Navajo man is longlimbed and relaxed, the Comanche has a war bonnet*, the dude has his quota of chaps and other pretensions, and his sombrero is inimitable. *Lily, who is less than two, attempts to sew beads along with her mother and her aunts.*

Although houses and some activities are modern, the newborn baby still lies with its mother on a bed of warm sand. That sand bed warmed many an ancient woman through her days of weakness, and her descendant prefers it to the iron bed which, perhaps, stands beside it. On the ground by the baby lies a perfect ear of corn, symbol of life, and beside his mother a divided one, symbol of fertility. The baby's ears must be pierced just as soon as possible and a bit of turquoise placed in them. Even if he be stillborn or if he die, the turquoise must not be omitted. If the baby lives, he must be taken out,

73

like all Pueblo babies, and presented to the Sun Father. His elders
sprinkle holy cornmeal while they say:

> Now this is the day.
> Our child
> Into the daylight,
> You will go out standing.
> . . . .
> Our child
> It is your day.
> This day
> The flesh of the white corn
> Prayer meal
> To our Sun Father
> This prayer meal we offer
> May your road be fulfilled
> Reaching to the road of your Sun Father.
> When your road is fulfilled
> In your thoughts (may we live)
> May we be the ones whom your thoughts will embrace
> For on this day
> To our Sun Father
> We offer prayer meal
> To this end
> May you help us all to finish our roads.

This presentation is equivalent to the baptism of the white people
and it is then that a baby receives its name. One should never ask a
Zuni child its name. You can find out if you must by asking a third
person; but Zuni like best to refer to a person as the brother of so
and so, or, better yet, of "the one who lives in that house".

Soon the child is hanging peacefully on its cradleboard watching
the room full of people who are its family. There is a grandmother

74

there, its mother's mother of course, for the father's parents are at home with their own daughters. The mother's sisters run in from their nearby houses and the child learns to call them all mother. Not that he does not know the difference, but the important thing is that they are all the women of his family, those to whose clan he belongs. For clan goes down in the female line in Zuni just as property does.

It gives the father, on the whole, a pleasant job. He pets and teaches the child and he certainly works to get him food. But suppose he should want a divorce—and divorce is as simple in Zuni as in the most ultra-modern of white cities—the result will not be a broken home. The home is the mother's and there she remains, with all the assistant mothers who are the baby's aunts. Grandfather and grandmother who are the real teachers remain too, and when a new father comes he will be kind and adaptable, like the former one. Zuni divorce is an interesting study for those who have the problem at heart. There is no blame attached; most of the troubles of the white man's system never existed, others are taken care of automatically.

There are men who always remain with the family, and those are mother's brothers, especially the oldest one. Of course they have families of their own, but they come home for all the ceremonies and family councils, and to them the child can always look for guidance and help. They are the men of his clan. If the family is a "valuable" one, guarding some of the sacred things brought from underground, they are priests. In a dark inner chamber where the child never goes they keep the venerated objects, and there his mother goes once a day to "feed" the holy things with cornmeal, removing her mocca-

75

sins at the door. When rain must be prayed for, the uncles enter that inner chamber and stay for four days, eight days or more, without meat or salt, while they roll thunder stones upon the floor and recite the sonorous words:

> That our earth mother
> May wear a fourfold green robe
> Full of moss,
> Full of flowers,
> Full of pollen...
> That our earth mother may wrap herself
> In a fourfold robe of white meal;
> That she may be covered with frost flowers;
> That yonder on all the mossy mountains
> The forests may huddle together with the cold.
> That their arms may be broken by the snow.

When the boy grows up he may be chosen to help them for they replace each dead priest by a new one from their own family. To be a member of a "valuable" family is the greatest thing in Zuni where men strive for material things through spiritual things.

Meantime he sees the masked gods dance in the plaza through all the summer months, for the kachinas visit Zuni as they do Hopi and no one can show in which they originated. When he is eight years old the fearful day comes when, in the mystery of the kiva, he is presented to them face to face. Again, when he is fourteen, he meets them and is told all their secrets. Now he is a man and he too may assume a mask and dance to bring the rain.

In fact, he must. The round of dances which are magic charms to keep the year on its course are not performed by the Zuni for pleasure.

76

Through a window a man.... may be seen bending over the delicate jewelry.... —→

Near the houses are the ...."*waffle-gardens*"*....*

— *Others carry water jars on their heads as of old....*

. . . . drive . . . . horses round and round . . . . till their hoofs have pounded out the grains.

Dancing is primarily a duty and in it there is great satisfaction, a feeling of having carried out an obligation well. Corn grows with hoeing and corn grows with the rain dances and no citizen must omit either one. We can hardly talk about the economic life of Zuni without its religion, or of religion without economics, for everything brings us back to corn.

The boy has been going to government school all this time and his teachers have kindly let him stay away for the periods of initiation and perhaps to help in the dances with those parts which children take. No one knows how he reconciles what he learns in physical geography with his own knowledge that the rain clouds are really the masked gods, summoned by Zuni dancing. He has not been very much with girls unless he is very modern, for girls have their own sphere of activities and boys theirs. Just because the house is so crowded, the psychological barriers between the sexes are made strong, and old fashioned Indian children would be astounded at the familiarity of white brothers and sisters; but a boy watches the girls as they go to the well and on the nights of great festivities when one may jostle and whisper in the crowd. He chooses his mate who is, of course, outside his clan, and that is all there is to it. The Hopi wedding involves demonstration of capacity on the part of groom and wife, as well as an exchange of gifts, the evidence of that capacity. Few tribes undertake marriage with as little ceremony as the ceremonious Zuni.

Ceremony or not, marriage is an important event for the shy boy, moving from home into a foreign household. He takes only his paints

77

and his dance kilt, and he goes to work with the other male in-laws of his new wife's household. The old Zuni civilization can take care of such crises. Everyone is polite and smiling; everyone makes room. Centuries of living in close quarters have taught the Zuni to keep their faces pleasant and their voices low. The gentle hum of their daily life is not broken by slaps or screams of anger, even by tiffs where housemates do not speak to each other. People may gossip in low tones where the offender does not hear, but the Zuni are utterly and constantly polite. If things get too bad, the marriage can break up. The invading husband picks up his kilt and paints and returns to his mother, or the wife may set his things outside and he can never come back. There is no social trouble for his wife, who can get another husband if she wants one.

Meantime the great duties of their lives go on. The man may have been chosen to perform an important rôle at one of the great ceremonies, and he must study and take offerings to the gods all year long. The woman has her children to care for, and, if her brothers are priests, she is often grinding the sacred cornmeal and cooking the special food which forms part of a ceremony. Neither lacks for social life, for the great feasts roll through the year in unending drama to which the whole town is invited. Every Zuni has a birthright membership in the society of men and gods.

When a marriage may break up at will, it often does not break, as students of the subject have found to their surprise. Often the husband takes deep root in the family and grows old with his children around him. Only then, after years of habituation, does he remove all his possessions to his wife's house and really call it home. If one of the married pair dies, the mourning may be extreme.

Death, to the Zuni as to so many Southwest Indians, is thought to be contagious and to cause other deaths by its mere presence. For that reason people avoid the dying, even their nearest and dearest, and never mention the names of the dead; but the widow or widower must take special precautions, since the dead mate was part of himself. For four days the widowed one used to sit alone, away from the fire, fasting from meat and salt and neither speaking nor being spoken to. Each day at dawn he went out to the east where he offered black corn-meal with his left hand to make the road dark for the ghost and white cornmeal with his right, while he prayed:

> My fathers,
> Our Sun Father
> Our mothers,
> Dawn
> As you arise and come out to your sacred place
> I pass you on your road
> The source of our flesh, white corn
> Shell, pollen,
> I offer to you...
> Sincerely from my heart,
> I send forth my prayers ...
> All of your good fortune whatsoever
> May you grant to us
> Preserving us along a safe road.
> May our roads be fulfilled.

To have his road fulfilled is all that the Zuni asks, for he has faith that the road is good. For the widower it leads to a year of seclusion

79

when all women must fear him. Then offerings to the gods and freedom from the ghost.

What are these offerings to the gods, with which Zuni life is interwoven? The Spaniards called them sacrifices and spoke of the unknown divinities as devils; but these beings are neither evil nor good, any more than the forces of Nature which they represent. There are many of them, but they are not organized into a family, like the gods of the Greeks and Romans, who parcelled out the affairs of the human race between father, mother, children, and step children. Zuni gods are of many different shapes and characters and, for all that mythology has to say, some of them do not even know each other. Perhaps many nations with their gods have combined in Zuni history. The tales of the way different groups came, one after one, each bringing its ceremony, are fewer than in Hopi. Though the Zuni have not thought it necessary to organize the gods, they have organized the ceremonies into a beautiful and artistic whole.

First among the gods is the sun, with his priest who counts the days until the solstices and tells the people when to make sun offerings of feathered prayer wands. Yet the sun priest did not come up with the people from underground as did the rain priests with their secret and sacred fetishes, kept in inner rooms and fed with cornmeal. Ever since the emergence, those fetishes have been kept in the same families, and once in winter and once in summer each priesthood retires to an inner room to fast and pray for rain for all the people. So they did underground, even in the fourth womb of the earth.

It was during their wanderings that some of their own children turned into beings who could bring the rain. They fell into a river and became water beings, but they can take human shape when they wish, and it is they who now dance and sing in the plaza on summer days, gorgeously dressed and masked. The Zuni call them kachinas as many other pueblos do. These gods, or ancestors or kachinas, live in a lake not far from Zuni and imagination riots in description of the dances and adventures which they have there. There are old wise kachinas and foolish young ones; there are ugly ones, beautiful ones and fierce ones. Each has his costume of cotton kilt or embroidered mantle or buckskin, decorations of parrot and eagle feathers, spruce boughs and fur; each has his peculiar cry.

They and the Zuni used to discuss together as to which ones would come to dance on sacred occasions; but, in legendary days, all that was settled. On special occasions like the solstice, their leader, Pautiwa appears, his face the color of turquoise, black about the eyes "like fine clouds that appear just before the sun rises", and ears large to hear everything his people say. Unlike many kachina he may speak and tell of his travels from the lake. Toward winter there comes the child god of fire, his black body painted with colored spots and behind him the tall creatures who run like great white fowls and who are the messengers of the kachinas, the Shalako. Sometimes to the merriment and fear of the people the mudhead clowns appear, having in their drum the black butterfly wings which make love magic so powerful that it is dangerous to deny them anything.

Off in the hills are the shrines of the war gods, twin children of the Sun, known to all the Southwest. The unwarlike Zuni have no dreadful tales about them but prefer to picture them as mischievous children, often scolded in old days by the town chief, but able to use arrows of lightning to help villagers in trouble. The Bow Priests hold for them their own secret ceremonies.

In the hills live the Beast Gods with power over sickness. The Zuni believe, like the Hopi, that animals have wonderful powers unknown to man; that they can send the most mysterious of ills and that they can cure it if properly invoked. Accordingly they have medicine societies which meet in secret chambers and sing until they have worked themselves into a state where they can achieve the power of the Bear, can place bear paws upon their hands and lay them on sick people to cure. Anyone can join these societies who has been cured by them and whose family can afford the expense. In general the four powerful animals are Mountain Lion, Wolf, Bear and Badger, the animals of the cardinal directions, north, west, south and east.

It is a strange collection of beliefs, culled perhaps from many parts of aboriginal America even as the white religion grew up out of Sumeria, Egypt, and Greece. Yet it has blended through the ages into a harmonious whole. Each supernatural being has a place in the calendar so that rain and war and curing are interwoven, all suffused with the gentle radiance of Zuni dance and song, offering of feathers and of cornmeal.

For such simple offerings are all that the supernaturals desire: feathers to adorn themselves and cornmeal to eat. Zuni women grind the cornmeal and mix it with powdered turquoise and white shell.

82

Women are the food givers, so they as well as the men scatter corn-meal before the fetishes. Men decorate painted wands with feathers:

> With the massed cloud wing
> Of the one who is our grandfather,
> The male turkey.
> With eagle's thin cloud wings,
> And with the striped cloud wings
> And massed cloud tails
> Of all the birds of summer.

It is done with ceremonial secrecy in the ceremonial chamber, and women never assist; but men make prayersticks for the women to plant. Thus the village continues in accord with the supernaturals, through gift and dance and song and prayer with fasting. These things all together make a magic formula which cannot fail. If no feather is wrong on the costume of a dancer, no word omitted from the long, traditional prayer, no rule broken while fasting, then blessing *must* come just as a seed must sprout after planting.

So think the Zuni, and in that conviction they have been at peace for century after century. Their villages have been ruled by Sun Priest and Rain Priests and Bow Priests meeting in council. A man has hunted or tilled his crops, danced in the plaza, prayed and made his prayersticks, and fought when he had to. A woman has ground her meal to feed both men and gods. For recreation, for emotional interest, and for spectacle they had their round of ceremonies or dances.

The dances go on. If the inner tubes of automobile tires sometimes replace earth-reddened buckskin, if Germantown yarn is substituted for strings of turquoise, does that mean that the essence of the ceremony has suffered? These things may in time become sacred as anything can that is used by a living religion. The wistful question of the white observer is whether this beautiful group unison, this manifold emotional satisfaction, is bound up by the mandate of history with the growing of corn by hand. Can none of it be brought over into a world of ploughs and machines and offices? How could the wisest Zuni do it? How could the wisest white man help him?

84

If she makes pots now she makes them for sale. ⟶

....the Navajo man is long-limbed and relaxed, the Comanche has a war bonnet....

— Somehow the art of sewing beads.... got started....

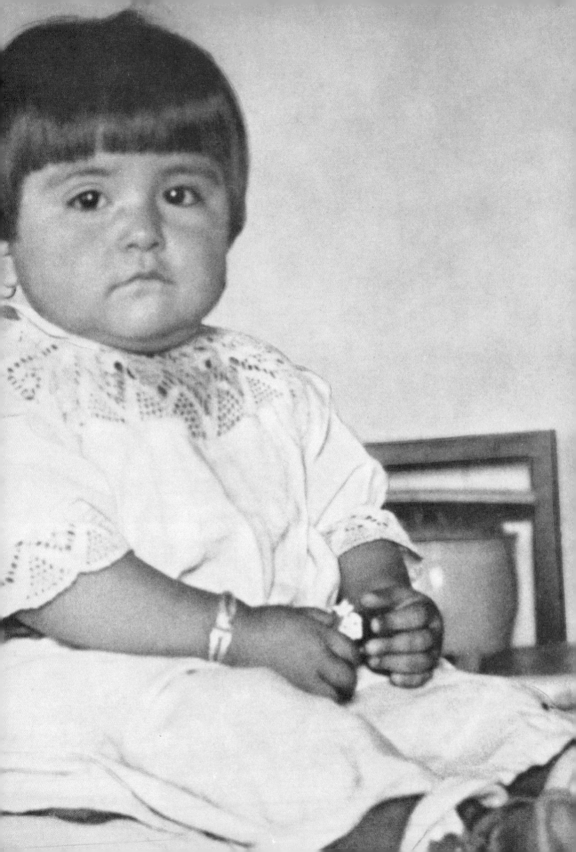

4

The Warriors of Keres

The Keresans were fighters. There is a breath of war in their ceremonies, war in their organization, war in their myths; war in their known history too. When the Spaniards came these villages did not save themselves by passive resistance or by springing back to the old life after every defeat. They fought. There are no more exciting pages in the history of New Mexico than the tale of the battle at Acoma, when the sky-city hurled its conquerors down from the cliffs and, since that did not stop them, cast down its own citizens, rather than submit.

There are seven towns of the Keres—Queres, if we use the old Spanish spelling: Acoma, Laguna, Zia, Santa Ana, San Felipe, Santo Domingo, and Cochiti. They lie eastward from Zuni as the red and gray desert turns to slopes dotted with juniper and then to valleys of

85

← Lily who is less than two years old attempts to sew beads along with her mother and her aunts.

cottonwood and alfalfa by the Rio Grande. Acoma and Laguna, perched among the low hills, are the first of them. Acoma with its flat roofs just showing above the great rock pedestal is the oldest inhabited town in the Southwest, after Oraibi of the Hopi. It is a hardy, desert town, a relic of old fighting days when the people lived for months with no water but that which settled in the rain reservoir on its summit, and were glad of the runlets from a tiny creek for their fields below. Laguna, whose flat roofs climb a hillside, like steps against the sky, is newer: a refugee town of Spanish days when people from many pueblos came there to find peace away from the river and the white armies. Its people speak a language similar to that of Acoma and the two, with the outlying farms, form a group by themselves, midway in many customs, between the western desert pueblos and the eastern ones by the river bank.

This way the Spaniards used to return when they had been, as they felt, almost to the western edge of the world and had carved their names on Inscription Rock. Before they were out of the desert they passed the high mesa where Acoma perched "like an island in the sky", "the strongest position that ever was seen in the world," and a landmark for the whole Southwest. They always stopped at the sky-city, going and coming. Or at least they always passed it; Acoma was not inviting to visitors.

It does not really invite them now but it suffers them—at a dollar a head. Leave your automobile at the mesa foot, for this is the one pueblo which cannot be reached by car. Climb up the steep footway which works the lungs of city dwellers almost to bursting. This is the

86

"new path"; the old one, where women once pulled themselves up by hand-and-foot holds from the spring in the valley below, was ruined by a fall of rock. At the head of the new path, where the flat rock juts out like a table top, you are greeted by a soft-voiced woman or even a child, the deputy sent by the war chief, to collect the fee.

Softly chattering, she leads the way along *winding, dusty paths, above which the terraced houses,* three and four storeys high, *are piled* like gray boulders. *Long ladders lead to the upper storeys.* Through their small windows you glimpse whitewashed walls and perhaps a niche with a saint's image. Here and there is a stove or a modern bed, but generally the old-fashioned Acomas of the mesa prefer the corner fireplace and the sheepskin on the floor. No women are grinding. The streets seem empty except for a dog or two and an old man sunning himself, *until suddenly we come upon a party repairing a house.* Out toward the edge of the cliff the piercing blue of the Southwest sky is mirrored in the reservoir of rain water which has kept Acoma alive through many a siege. The bell from the old adobe church echoes over land which seems empty of all but cloud shadows.

"Where are the people?"

"They stay down below on their farms."

A watcher might not know unless he was told that the patches of brown among the cloud shadows are the roofs of little square farm houses scattered along irrigation ditches. The Acoma have had ditches along with their dry farming almost since the first Spaniards arrived. They used to run down to their patches of land as the Hopi do, and their maidens used to clamber down to the distant spring, always

87

coming back to the mesa top; but in recent years the stays in the valley have grown longer and longer. Why go back to the mesa for winter? Why not build a house? Clusters of houses have grown up, four of them all together, with a school and a church. Sometimes in summer the war chief finds himself alone on the rock with his deputies. The sky-city is moving down.

So is its next door neighbor, Laguna. Above the gas station on the road its gray roofs rise like rock ledges against the blue southwestern sky but they shelter fewer and fewer people. The need for such a refuge is past, and down in the valley spread Laguna's eight daughter villages, from large Mesita to tiny "New York". They are raising chili and alfalfa for sale: they are keeping sheep, goats, and cattle. Acoma and Laguna were picturesque survivals until a few years ago but, with their outward move, they have jumped to first rank among pueblo farmers. Old methods were left behind on the hilltop, and now they are ready for tools and farming practises very different from those of seventeenth century Spain long used by their kinsmen.

When we leave this halfway station we see in the distance the gleam of water. Here through the desert country winds the bright green ribbon of the Rio Grande valley, frayed into tributary streams, in whose moist coves the corn grows like grass. This is the home of the other Keres. Above Jemez Creek perch Zia and Santa Ana, their fields at their feet. In the lush valley of the Rio Grande, the Great River itself, lie the spreading fields of San Felipe, Santo Domingo and Cochiti. The very saint names tell us that this way the Spaniards passed. Yet these are not Spanish towns. Despite the irrigated fields, the separate houses with strings of chili hanging beside the doors, despite the church and the new and gleaming school, these are some of the most tenaciously Indian of any towns in New Mexico. As white civilization pressed close around their undefended fields, they fought, not with guns, but with secrecy. Those who spoke of their gods as devils and treated their customs either with ridicule or suppression were kept out by a psychological barrier, the only one left. While Hopi and Zuni receive with a smiling tolerance the bus-loads of Whites which journey to their ceremonies, Keresan villages often post guards on the hilltops to turn visitors away. Domingo asks even the government officials to leave town. They fought for their integrity in the old days; they are still fighting.

How came such a people to live in the good corn country while those whose very life is focussed upon their crops are marooned in the western desert? The anthropological sleuths suggest that those others never knew about the Rio Grande. They came out of the west, north, or south and settled at what is to us a day's journey from the river, to them many weeks venturing into the unknown. Perhaps, even so, they were in better land than they had left.

There were no settlements at all on the Rio Grande, say the diggers, until the great pueblo culture was already failing and its cities were moving east before the onslaught of the wanderers. That was about 1300 A.D.—late for the Southwest. Were the Keres old pueblo dwellers, who moved because of drought and enemies and luckily found the fertile river bottom? The scattered pottery scraps, the reference book for this fascinating prehistory, say they may have come down

89

from the cliff houses of Colorado. Or did the Keres move in from the plains at the east, the mountains at the north, or the varied and populous country of Mexico at the south? Did they meet pottery-making people and learn from them? In spite of all the study being eagerly carried on in the Southwest, these questions are not yet answered, and even the relationship of the Keresan language is still in doubt. That language is a hard nut to crack, with queer "frozen" forms, as though the English *I am, you are, he is*, had turned forever into *I be, you be, he be*. It might do that if the backwoods farmers who use it were cut off permanently from the rest of their countrymen, and perhaps these Keresans were cut off from the main body of their people.

All they have to tell us is the mysterious underground story. They wandered to a place called the White House, where they met people who taught them all they know. (There is a ruined "White House" now in northern Arizona but this scattering of names is nothing to take seriously.) However, it is interesting to see how early wanderings in the Southwest glimmer through all these stories. No tribe has a solitary history but each met some other tribe and learned from it. Then the story brings us to the Rio Grande country and there, indeed, we can pick out the ruined sites which the Keres say were once theirs. The most dramatic tale, as usual, is that of Acoma. *The villagers point to the cliff, called by Whites the Enchanted Mesa.* There, they say, they once lived until a crumbling of the rock destroyed their only path and no one could go up or down. Most of them were in the fields at the time, but several old people were on the mesa. They stayed there and died.

By the time the Spaniards arrived the travels of the Keres were over and the villages were very nearly where they are now. Not quite. Acoma is the only one which has not moved or been deserted. It received the first visitors peacefully, since they came in small parties and did not stay long. It was a different thing when Don Juan de Oñate was finally appointed Governor and Captain General and made the tour of the pueblos, requiring their submission. Zuni and Hopi already had a taste of gunpowder by that time and they submitted— at least in word; but Acoma, on its four hundred foot rock, with its stores of corn and its rain reservoirs, felt its powers. First the inhabitants tried to lure the Captain General down into a kiva and murder him. Subsequently, when a party of his men were strutting about the cliff top, the natives fell upon them with clubs and yells and killed all who did not jump off.

Spain had to avenge that, and the tale of her revenge is told in blank verse composed by one of the soldiers. Our translation of Villagrá's hendecasyllabics is a little like what the Spanish censor said of the verse itself: "lacking in imagination and poetical worth but a true and connected history".

The Spanish sergeant and his little force, says Villagrá, gathered under the mesa wall, considering how to attack it or how to climb up. The two hundred fighting men of the Acoma looked down and, knowing that their arrows would never pierce those leather jackets and steel corselets,

> "Of stones, they did let loose such a great torrent
> As falls when storm breaks forth from the high heaven
> With thunder after frightful roar of thunder
> And with the force of lightning to dismay us."

But even stones had little effect on the Spanish armor and

> Astounded, the barbarians looked down then
> And saw, unharmed, the marvellous Castilians.

Meanwhile some chosen Spaniards had scaled the mesa by a back way, crossed a chasm on a log, and fallen upon the villagers from behind. These soldiers had swords.

> And thus the fighters opened bloody fountains
> In the barbarians, ribs and breasts and bodies.
> Their eyes, their heads, their gullets all were flowing
> With streams of their own blood, fresh and abundant
> And from their wounds, so hideously gaping,
> Their frightened souls were very nearly fleeing.

Then the Spaniards from below fired the cannon which they had dragged all the way from Mexico. The Indians ceased yelling. Like a flock of frightened magpies when a shotgun has been fired among them:

> Thus did we see them, all the dead and dying
> Crippled or handless, slashed in two or halting
> Their breasts torn open, hideously wounded
> Heads gashed, arms torn through in a thousand places
> Pouring out living blood as, agonizing,
> They sent forth their immortal souls and left there
> Upon the ground their palpitating corpses.

The Spanish sergeant called on the Indians to surrender and promised to treat them all with mercy and justice as if he were their own father. They replied that, rather than submit, they, their wives, and children would perish at their own hands. "And they fought so hard that it caused the attackers great grief."

Three days the battle went on while the Spaniards had no chance to eat, sleep, or even sit down:

92

Meantime he sees the masked gods dance in the plaza.... ⟶

. . . . winding dusty paths above which the terraced houses . . . . are piled.

Long ladders lead to the upper storeys. ——

. . . . *until suddenly we come upon a party repairing a house.*

Nor let their weapons from their hands, still shedding
Such blood that they were drowned and sick and weary
Of shedding blood. And then a fire sent forth
Its flaming smoke, till one after another,
The wretched houses burned. And still it mounted
Through the dry, pitchy pine of all the dwellings
Catching the log roofs in a thousand places
Till, from the windows, issued, slowly rolling
A thick, dense smoke, like wool. Now here, now yonder,
As from the mouths of fiery volcanoes
Flew up a mass of sparks and flakes of fire.

Then the barbarians, furious and vanquished,
Seeing their fate, did turn to kill each other.
The father slew the son, the son the father
And others turned to help the raging fire
To burn more fiercely and consume the pueblo
Embraced in flames.

Villagrá's "accurate" account even recites the speech of the bravest
Acoma chieftain when the others tried to dissuade him from committing suicide. Life would be infamous without liberty, he told
them, and such words must really have been said, though perhaps
not in Villagrá's Roman sounding words. For the Acoma kept their
promise to die rather than surrender.

Not Nero, or the other cruel tyrants,
E'er seemed more terrible, or more atrocious
Than these barbarians toward one another.
And not the braves alone, but women also.
Some slew themselves, like Dido, and the fire
Consumed their bodies, while their Spartan children
Sought, like their mothers, a grim death, while others
Threw themselves in the raging flames. Some mothers

93

Clasping their children, leaped from the high summit.
. . . .
Many, in different ways, found death.

The survivors made peace. The Governor and Captain General held a meeting of all the Keres at Domingo, where important meetings are still held. He wanted them, he said, to submit to the king of Spain, but he was particularly anxious for the salvation of their souls. They submitted.

All of them in time were organized like Spanish villages, at least as far as the Spaniards could see. Each had a church where a priest came every Sunday, and three had convents. *Acoma's church is still standing*, perched near the edge of the precipice and upheld by ancient timbers which the Acoma dragged from the distant mountains. In its courtyard are the peach trees, kept alive by water which, they say, they were forced to give from their cherished rain reservoirs, *and below it are corrals in which burros are kept*. Even the most sanguine reporters never dared speak of Acoma as fully Christian. "It is being catechised" they said, but all the other Keres were baptized and going to school. They were very good, reported the Commissary General, at reading, writing and instrumental music.

What were they thinking as they tilled their little farms and often the Spanish farms too, as they went to be catechised, decently clothed in calico shirts and dresses? An old story which may date from that far off time comments on the new supernatural who seemed a sort of kachina, like the masked beings who brought the rain. The white men called him God. Once, says the story, he entered into a contest with one of the old Keresan kachinas.

94

"Let us both shoot at a tree," they proposed, "and see who does best."

So God shot with a gun but the kachina with lightning. The kachina split the tree.

Then they compared the sort of food they had to eat. God sat at a table with lots of good things. The kachina sat on the ground with venison and tortillas and enjoyed them so much that God came and joined him.

Then they both undertook to bring water for the crops. God wrote a letter but, while someone was reading it, the kachina took prayer feathers and brought rain.

They tried a musical contest. God blew a horn and the kachina sang to a drum. Then God got tired and went away on a cloud, the kachina on the back of a duck.

That expressed the situation for the Keres but not for the Christians. Earnest missionaries objected strongly to the underground houses where the Indians "made offerings to the devil", and these houses of idolatry were burned. There may be a reason why the Keres never allow a white person to enter their kivas or to see their masked dances. Even the most careless word, spoken about them to an outsider, is disloyalty to the pueblo.

Then 1680 came and the meekly singing converts were turned into furies. The Keres killed their priests and burned their churches. Then they fled to the hills and waited for vengeance to burst on them. Or most of them did. Zia and Santa Ana, the smallest, could not put up much resistance, but legend has it that it was a wounded Zia chief who finally pried out of His Majesty's government the land grants which have been treasured by the pueblos ever since. They were made in 1689, while the Spanish officials were in refuge at El Paso del Norte, now in Texas. The story goes that the Zia man assured Spain that if each pueblo had its land secured to it in fee simple, there would be no more fighting. The grants were given and Spain came back three years later but most of the pueblos were deserted. Acoma had felt safe enough on her citadel "the best in existence among Christians" but Domingo, San Felipe and Cochiti were camping on a mesa top with a few frightened villages of the Tewa. Even when De Vargas appeared, promising to be a father to them, the Cochiti refused to come down. As the weaker villages one by one went home or gave in, she and Santo Domingo pounced down and fought them, but ultimately the Spanish governor captured some three hundred of their women and children whom he distributed as slaves. That ended it.

Even the "traitors, enemies, rebels and apostates" of Acoma made peace and were absolved of their sins. Some of them had to be killed finally because their idea of peace was not very permanent but by and large the rebellion was over. The Pueblos went back to tilling their fields and another enemy took care of Spain without their knowing it. In 1823 New Mexico was taken over by the United States of Mexico; in 1848 by the "United States of the North". In 1912 it became one of those states.

Through all this the Keres had one concern, their land. They had bargained with the Spaniards to get their little grants—two miles

96

and a half, theoretically, in every direction from the church. They bargained with the new government. They would not fight, they told the first agent, in the 1850's, either with the Spanish Americans or with the wild Navajo, if only they might be protected in their land. Congress renounced all claim to consider their land public property and gave them quitclaim deeds. The Pueblos of New Mexico are the only Indians in the United States to hold land in this way. Congress did not consider them citizens, even though every one else taken over from Mexico had that status if he wanted it. Those were the days when all Indians were thought to be alike, and the United States had no knowledge of the old civilizations brought within its borders.

Abraham Lincoln came nearest to recognizing them. He sent to each pueblo in New Mexico canes of office for the governor and lieutenant governor, each with the president's name on a silver plate. Any officer photographed can generally be seen holding his Lincoln cane. The mills of government, grinding with god-like slowness, ultimately produced a gift of tools for the pueblos and a few extra reservations of land.

There were Indian agents, first for all New Mexico, later for groups of pueblos. There were a few day schools and two impressive boarding schools. There was no recognition of the problems of a civilized people, struggling in isolation in the midst of a foreign civilization. Herds ate the grass from pueblo lands, settlers took the water, and new diseases killed as many people as the Spanish swords. The Indian Commissioner reported that the New Mexico Pueblos were dying out and two were nearly gone already.

97

It was not until after the World War that Congress really considered the Pueblos. They found that settlers had moved in on their land, and that, to keep faith with their wards, they owed them some millions of dollars either in land or money. They promised to pay. The Pueblos have some of the money already and they have spent it for land, for tools, and for ditches owned by the whole village. Now there is a superintendent for all the pueblos except distant Hopi. There are four hospitals and nine or ten doctors, besides the trim field nurses, willing to drive a car over any rocky road at any hour. The population has begun to increase, and in some villages it has doubled and tripled since Lincoln's day.

Has that population changed its desires or the customs that shape them? Keresan children held pretty firm through the Spanish catechizing, through the first American day schools, and the big boarding schools where children, all clad alike in calico frocks or gray sweaters, marched docilely to meals of pork and potatoes. "Centuries might roll away," wrote one of the agents, "and the posterity of this people would remain essentially the same." He was objecting because a way of living, instilled into every memory and emotion, does not change with five or six years of boarding school. Ultimately that fact got itself admitted and the pueblos blossomed with clean little day schools, with workrooms and laundries for the mothers, and a teacher glad to be a neighbor. Keresan children up to the age of thirteen have just as much schooling as white children, say Government reports. After that if they like they can go to High School, to a special vocational school, or with a government loan, to college. Their real life is still

98

in the pueblo however, and they hearken to the village council which bids them not to stay away too long; not to marry outside the pueblo; to come home for the ceremonies, the community work, the life, once all absorbing, which the village is fighting to keep intact.

But even the village has changed from former days. Gone are the old terraced houses and two storeys are the most you will see. Most of the little adobe dwellings, with painted window and door frames, look very like those of the Spanish Americans in the neighboring fields. In modern towns like San Felipe, they seem all like that but in Cochiti they still crowd closely around the plaza where ranks of shawled women stand to watch the rain dances. Zia and Santa Ana are still perched on bleak hills, but only theoretically. Santa Ana has moved down to the riverside, leaving a man or two to watch the pueblo. Zia has new fields across the river; Laguna has spread into nine farming villages and Acoma into four. Only Domingo, the unofficial capital of the Keres, remains barricaded between its network of horse corrals and its rich fields, the largest on the Rio Grande.

In all of them babies are still presented to the sun. Boys, in the intervals of going to school, till the fields, herd the horses, and clean the irrigation ditches. Girls sweep the whitewashed rooms and gather the sleeping rugs from the floor to hang on the "pole of the soft goods" which is the cupboard. Dressed sometimes in moccasins and dark blue *manta*, or in flowered frocks with high-heeled slippers, they bend over fireplace or stove, serve canned beef or corn meal. You can find any combination somewhere among the Keres.

Often they trot busily to the heap of smoking cow dung where pots

99

are firing, for many Keres women are commercial potters. In the gray dawn they may leave the earthen floored pueblo room to tramp in their moccasins, backs bent under a blanket full of pots, to that point where the emptiness of the New Mexico hills is suddenly cut by the smooth solidity of the transcontinental road. There for twenty feet is the atmosphere of a city; there cars stop laden with people of every costume and every accent in the United States. *The women, children* and even men of the pottery villages *sit under shelters* made of four crooked posts and a roof of branches, holding up their pots with a smiling invitation far more courteous than the advertising methods of the Whites. They must know more than any other Indians about the inhabitants of the United States, but they return to the pueblo— or they do in this generation.

Their living has to be on a pueblo scale, for pots that cost more than a dollar do not appeal to tourists, so the women finish a pot less carefully than in the old days and give it a shape for decoration and not for use. One can still recognize the tall vases of Zia with the bird, the large red flower, the great swooping band called the line of the sky, the rain symbols of Cochiti; the bold triangles of Santo Domingo, black on a cream ground; and the finely tempered, squat jars of Acoma, with their profusion of red and black triangles.

Most of the other arts have gone. Women gave up basketry in Spanish days and a generation ago they gave up weaving; for among the Keres women wove. They learned for a while from the Spaniards about steel needles for embroidery and brilliant colored wools. Each garment they made in those days was simply a square or oblong, tied

The villagers point to the cliff called by the Whites the Enchanted Mesa.

somehow about the body; but when they began to wear fitted clothing, they bought the Spaniard's calicos, even his silks and velvets. What weaver would have the heart to slash the threads she herself had woven! Only in ceremonies do the kilts and blankets appear now, and they are bought from the Hopi.

The Keres have something to trade for them, or at least those of Domingo do. They make jewelry with turquoise mountings or with the smooth gloss of old phonograph records substituted for the ancient jet. Their men wander far and wide selling these, or buckskins, or the clay for pottery, and it is no uncommon sight to see a Domingan on a city street, his hands loaded with Zuni rings, his shoulder with Navajo blankets, and in one hand a sackful of Domingo pots, all for sale. White traders say they are the ablest bargainers in all New Mexico. Yet these shrewd merchants are not being weaned from their village. They are in business, not so they can get away from pueblo life, but so they can go back to it. The white farm boy, dazzled by his trips to town, is far less sophisticated than these ancient village dwellers, who know a great deal about other ways of life but choose their own.

The old life of the pueblo goes on, not unconsciously, but with planned intent. All men are still required to labor at work on the irrigation ditches or at herding the horses. In the same way men and women too, must dance when the rain is being called down or pay a fine. No one must marry outside the pueblo and, from some of them, no one must stay away for very long without permission of the officials. No one must tell the sectrets of the pueblo or, in fact, give any in-

◄— Acoma's church is still standing. . . .

formation at all. No one must act in a spirit contrary to that of the community. No one must get drunk or cause internal dissensions. The Keresans enforce their own law and order without calling on the white man.

Life goes on behind doors closed tight with apprehension. No White would do it the discourtesy to pry needlessly into the exact sequence of hunt dances which once brought game to the pueblo; corn dances which brought germination and rain and harvest; rituals of the solstice which kept the sun on its course and those of curing societies which ensured health and increase. However, between these ancient ceremonies with which we are already familiar, are interspersed such combinations of the new and old as dancing in the church on Christmas day; making clay figurines of animals with a prayer for increase; carrying pots of old-style food to the dead at All Souls; dancing for Santiago, San Pedro and San Esteban or honoring San Juan in the mediaeval Spanish manner with a troop of galloping horsemen striving to pull a live rooster from the ground. Perhaps we should add Christian baptism, marriage (sometimes) and burial. There is proof enough that the old religion has made a place among its own supernaturals for Dios, the Virgin, and the saints.

No one would doubt it who had seen the spectacle of the Domingo corn dance, goal of half the visitors to the Southwest. Through the clever adaptation of past Franciscan missionaries it takes place on the day of Saint Dominic, for whom the town is named. The saint is brought from the church under a canopy of branches and carried through the village as in the religious processions of old Spain. Guns are fired, as were the arquebuses in the seventeenth century, and the saint is placed under a leafy bower from which, amid his offerings, he can watch the measured beauty of the dance for rain.

In solemn file the dancers issue from the great circular kiva which stands partly above ground, not sunk or hidden as in Hopi and Zuni. The long black hair, wavy from previous tight braiding, floats about the bare torsos of men and the ancient woven mantles of women. Red circles on the cheek bones, under the fixed eyes and the straight bang of black hair, lend vividness to each dark face. The women's heads are topped with upright slabs of latticed wood and feathers, like those of Hopi kachinas or the warriors of Mexico and Yucatan; their shapely feet are bare on the hot rocks. The men are magnificent in colored moccasins, embroidered kilt, fringed sash of ancient cotton, a dangling fox skin at the back and an armor of turquoise jewelry. D. H. Lawrence, in describing such a dance, made an Indian say; "The men are the stars and the women are the dark spaces between the stars." Around them posture the sacred clowns, striped in dead black and gray and coiffed with withered corn husks. A choir of old men in Spanish finery bounces gently like a buoy on the ocean as they sing to the dancers' rattles.

Keresan women belong to the kivas and all must dance in their turn. Even without mishandling their veil of secrecy, we can see striking differences between the Keres and the western Pueblos. No powerful mother clans. Clans seem faint, almost passing; and instead there are generally two kivas. Squash and Turquoise, they are usually called, and it is from the kivas that the corn dancers come alternately at intervals all day long. Everyone belongs to Squash or Turquoise according as his father did, for in kiva membership descent has gone back to the system looked upon as natural by the Whites.

The government is priestly still, but different. Among the priestly rulers of Hopi and Zuni offices are passed down in the family, along with the sacred objects brought from underground. The Keres are ruled by medicine societies whose membership is voluntary. Any man may come to be the highest priest of all by joining a society and rising to be its oldest or most important member. There are several medicine societies and one of them furnishes the high priest whom the Spaniards called cacique. They brought that word, by the way, from the West Indies, but the pueblo people themselves now use it proudly.

This high priest, gentle, reflective, forbidden to quarrel, is the power behind a Keresan town, with a war captain or two to do the active work and a council to advise him. Usually the Whites know nothing of this ancient government, functioning vigilantly still. For the Keres have dutifully appointed governors ever since they were required to do so by the Laws of the Kingdoms of the Indies. The governor and his assistants and the church officers form a parallel government, changing every year and dealing only with business and the Whites, but the governor has found a real place in village life, just as the saints have. One who believes that Indians never change can be easily contradicted by the sight of these Spanish customs grown smoothly into the texture of Indian life.

Laws and schools do not make the lasting, irrevocable changes.

These come from livelihood, just as they did when the pueblo people first moved into this country to raise their food. They found they had to settle down and on that settling down followed houses, village government and ceremonies with a fixed date. These things built themselves up because of the land which gave corn. Now there is a change in that land. It is not inexhaustible. Only a short time ago the Whites awoke to the fact that the bosom of Nature, over which they had roamed so freely since the days of Columbus, was drying up. Cutting down trees and sending out herds of animals to nibble off the grass is not the treatment it requires, so the Whites have been planting green things again and restricting their herds. Now they have put the matter up to the Indians.

It is an interesting thing to see the men of a pueblo community gathered in council. They sit, no longer on sheepskins, but on benches in a white plastered community house. The blue jeans which every Indian wears nowadays blend with the blue tobacco smoke, through which appear serious faces, bent thoughtfully as they have been for hours. They wish to understand the arguments and to have every man know all the facts. White farmers who have protested furiously about having their liberty interfered with, just because the soil must be conserved, are surprised at the reasonable acquiesence of the Indians. Several of the Keres and their next door neighbors, the Tewa, have entered into an eight year agreement with the government. They agree to conform to its plan for bringing back the soil, and to cut down their herds year by year. This means that Laguna, for intance, reduces its sheep from 50,000 to 15,000. In return, the government will fence for them and plant cover to hold the soil and advise them where and when to pasture.

It is a modern partnership between White and Indians, and the first which has had any importance from the Indian point of view. When the White speaks, not about the best way to marry or worship, but about the best way to make a living, the Indian listens. And he may find that the new plans carry with them as many consequences as the discovery of corn, which changed wanderers to village dwellers. For the new use of land means the end of unscientific primitive agriculture. It is too wasteful in a crowded country. There must be modern tools and ditches regulated by modern mechanism. That means expense. That means cash crops. The pueblos, which up to now have succeeded in working and trading almost without money, are coming to need more and more cash.

For the last few years they have had cash in what, to them, was revolutionary quantity. Indian Emergency Conservation Work employed almost every able-bodied man for some days a mouth. All but the men of Santo Domingo. The most conservative town of the Keres and their unofficial capital refused this comparative wealth. Was there any other town in America that did so? The others had had a taste of the life of the modern wage worker. How is this going to affect handicraft, subsistence farming, a village life sufficient unto itself? Thoughtful Indians, young and old, are considering this problem which has to be solved by their own choice. The government stands ready to use its machinery of schools and loans, not to drag them out of their villages, but to make their life there dignified, self supporting, an asset to the country around them which knows all too little of rural content or cooperative enterprise. America, in its post-depression thinking spell, has been preaching the value of these things and has found they cannot be acquired over night. Here they are in full, possessions so common to the Pueblo Indians that they are hardly noticed. The problem for Indians and Whites is to bring them over undamaged into the new partnership and to help them grow.

....and below it are corrals.... ——

. . . . in which burros are kept. . . .

. . . . the women, children . . . . sit under shelters. . . .

Catholic . . . . they were in much sincerity. . . .

5

The Catholic Tewa

Heart and life of the Southwestern world in Spanish days was the Rio Grande Bravo del Norte: Great Wild River of the North. Its cultivated valley still paints desert New Mexico with one long streak of green, from north to south. Its shallow waters gleam crimson and brown and purple between streaks of liver-colored mud. Heavy with the soil they have washed away, they flood in ripples, eating at their banks, piling up shoals or crumbling the earth from under buildings. From those banks run the irrigation ditches whose water gurgles among the corn and the alfalfa and into neat rows of chili, onions, wheat and fruit which grow thick in the hot fields. This was the ancestral land of the Tewa.

Peaceful or not, civilized or not, there was only one future for Indians who occupied the valley of the one large river in New Mexico.

They had to accept the Spaniards. Had they fought like the Acoma they would simply have been extinguished. To try evasion, like the Hopi, would have been laughable. As a result, the Tewa speak Spanish almost as much as Indian. They sow, reap and go to church like their Spanish American neighbors who live on the Pueblo grants and even in the pueblos themselves. The clean little adobe houses in fields and plaza, with their whitewashed walls and saint's pictures might be, to outward appearance, either Spanish-American or Indian.

Further acquaintance would change that impression, for the Tewa have kept to many of their ancient ways, fighting, like the other Pueblos, with the only weapon left to them, that of secrecy. They have had three hundred years of wheat and horses and white man's irrigation; of calico, tin and shoe leather, of church instruction and written law. A Tewa in these days remains Indian only by choice. He has the background, if he wishes, to be a teacher, an artist, an engineer, a businessman and some have so chosen. The story of that adaptation is a long one.

The Tewa speak a language which is called Tanoan and it has more divisions than any other group in the Southwest. Visitors struggle with the difference between Tewa, Tigua (pronounce it Teewa) and Towa, each belonging to several villages which express genuine surprise when the white grammarian insists that they must all be related. In ancient days there were even more, for the Spaniards found the Piro and the Tano who have long since disappeared. Once this great group of peoples with languages related perhaps as English, French, and German are related, stretched down the Rio Grande,

from Taos near the border of Colorado into Texas. That was somewhere about the fourteenth century, time of the Renaissance in Europe.
It seems long ago to the white man, but actually it was late in Pueblo
history. By that time villages had already risen and fallen in the Hopi
country and the pueblo people were moving east before the nomads.

Here we find one of the most intriguing gaps in Southwestern
history. Were these Tanoans of the Great River old pueblo dwellers
who moved to new country? If so, their flight was a blessing when it
brought them out of the mountains and deserts into a luxurious valley
never settled before. But why are the ruins and the pottery so crude?
Were the people hurried and frightened or had they among them new
immigrants coming from a wilder life? One student has found a
likeness in the Tanoan language to that of the fighting Kiowa of the
eastern Plains. No records of this hidden history except scattered
scraps of pottery to be traced step by step through Arizona, Colorado
and New Mexico, or knotty grammatical forms which need comparison
with half the languages in America!

The Spaniards found the Tanoans in the valley of the Great River,
that coveted valley which constituted for two hundred and twenty
five years the actual domain of His Majesty in New Mexico. There
were fifty villages or so in those days: Piro, Tano, Tigua, Towa and
Tewa. Their terraced houses, their fields of corn, beans and pumpkins, and their flocks of turkey filled the valley of the Rio Grande and
spread up the Jemez and the Chama and out into the plains with
only the little group of the Keres to interrupt the long chain somewhere above Albuquerque.

III

These pages cannot follow the story of the vanished Tano and the Piro, snuffed out, one by one, as the Apache moved closer. Jemez and Pecos of the Towa, Sandia and Isleta of the once great province of Tiguex (Tigua, Tiwa) have long histories which cannot be told here. Our concern is the group of Tewa in the center of the Rio Grande valley. Eight of them tilled their fields there once, and now there are six: San Juan, Santa Clara, San Ildefonso, Nambe, Tesuque, Pojoaque. The last was reduced a few years ago to one person, but now some of the emigrants have come back and it is growing again, as they all are. Their population all together comes to nearly a thousand, with four hundred and twenty six in San Juan, the largest village.

Coronado had to do some exploring before he found the Tanoans, for he did not suspect the existence of the Rio Grande. When his men arrived there they stayed, so the valley dwellers got their lesson early. The Spaniards wintered on the Rio Grande at a place they called Tiguex, and so the Tigua people learned that they should not resent the assaulting of an Indian woman or the commandeering of clothing, even off their backs. They and Pecos of the Towa out toward the Plains tried the scheme of luring the terrible visitors out into the country, "level like the sea", to see the humpbacked cattle and, of course, to find gold. It did not work. The doughty conquistadores came back alive but angry, and the Tigua had to feed them for another winter. By the time the next explorers came the Indians were well trained.

Spanish parties after that always came up the Rio Grande. But the first arrivals were not interested in colonizing. For a time only

112

priests and soldiers came and went—or stayed and were killed. Then came the end of the sixteenth century when the furor of discovery was over and every big European power was making its bid for land. Spain established the province of New Mexico.

In 1598 Don Juan de Oñate, first Governor and Captain General, came marching up the valley of the Great River with flocks and tools and colonists, looking for a place to settle. He pitched upon a Tewa village, Cuyamungue. San Juan de los Caballeros (St. John of the Gentlemen) he called it, and San Juan it remains to the present day. Legend disputes as to whether the gentlemen were the Conquistadores or the Tewa who moved out of their houses to let the conquerors in.

The Spaniards built themselves a capital called San Gabriel across the river and managed there in Indian style houses until the old city of Santa Fe got its start in 1605. They had a garrison there, fed by Indian corn which the "fierce Tehua" were supposed to contribute gratis. They did. What other recourse had they in their undefended villages, and what had the Spaniards, needing corn and help against the nomads? The missionaries went in; the churches went up. In 1630 the General Supervisor of New Mexico Missions reported all the Tewa baptised, to the number of 6000 souls. There was a church in every one of the villages, that of San Ildefonso being especially beautiful, and Tewa of many ages were going to school. They were paying for their own education with taxes of corn and buckskin and the fiscales were taking tithes for the priests. For all the villages had fiscales, governors, lieutenant governors, and sheriffs. All were baptised, married and

113

buried, by the priest — if he got hold of them. All went to mass once a week on pain of a whipping.

"They are the first nation to be baptised," said the report, "of which they are very proud. They are very friendly to Spain, whom they help in all her wars. They are well taught in the arts. They have fertile land and the priest has introduced irrigation." Thus began that close contact of the Tewa and the Whites which has lasted until the present day, interrupted only by those famous twelve years which are known as the first American revolution.

The Tewa watched the Spaniards move in along the Rio Grande and plant orchards, vegetable gardens, and wheat fields. There were grants as large as whole townships and counties where the irrigation ditches gurgled and the Indians could watch the threshing of wheat with horses, the growing of chili from Mexico, and of grapes from Spain. They were servants in the great houses, could see the ladies in silk dresses and the horses with silver trappings, for the Oñate grantees and their descendants were "empowered to do all the things done by the knights of Castille and enjoy all their privileges".

Even the remote villages had a chance to learn the white man's ways and to get on the government payroll at one *real* (thirteen cents) per day. It is in memory of this ancient currency that the Southwest still speaks of twenty-five cents as two bits. San Ildefonso one year made 263 pairs of stockings for the governor's store; San Juan and Nambe, with other Tewa villages now gone, made 280. Most of the Tewa hauled wood and got, instead of their *real*, lengths of calico or pots or bullets, since real money was scarce in the new country. With great

114

labor or cleverness they might earn horses or they might steal them if they could somehow disguise the fact that all the horses of his Majesty's government had one ear cut off.

All this should have seemed a privilege, but it turned out later that the Indians all this time were wishing for nothing but to get back to their old life "which", said the surprised investigator, "was the best they could hope". What they wanted was plenty of corn, squash, beans—and peace. *Catholic* though *they were in much sincerity, they had kept their ancient ceremonies* on condition that these should be supervised by the priests and purged of everything idolatrous. The priests, they found, were likely to consider almost everything idolatrous. The Tewa, who had been hospitable to the Christian God, objected to having their own sacred kivas called "houses of idolatry, rape and obscenity". The fantastic and mysterious disguise of their dancing gods did not seem to them "very ugly masks which are an imitation of the devil".

Spain noticed the restlessness of the Indians and word came from the viceroy of Mexico that there was to be no more cutting of Indians' hair, since that made them leave the pueblos. Nor were they to be forced to carry heavy loads or to have Spanish horses trample their cornfields with impunity. A council even met to decide if they might not keep their native dress. But "when cancer moves about in the body there is no security for the heart". When there is discontent in an Indian village, Spanish authorities had best be firm. They were. Indians were flogged faithfully for getting drunk or failing to go to church and for many offenses besides. For misdemeanors somewhat

worse, they could be sold as slaves. Now and then one of them murdered a Spaniard. Four of them were hanged for this reason about
1675 and forty-three were sold into slavery. There was talk of their
having used witchcraft. Several more were in jail in Santa Fe and the
Tewa came, threatening to flee to the mountains if they were not
released. One of the prisoners, say the accounts, was an old man named
Popé.

He was the enemy of the government from that time, and the
government rued its treatment of him. He came from San Juan, where
his son-in-law was the governor, and the Indians reported later that
he killed the son-in-law lest he interfere with his plans. For Popé
planned nothing less than a general uprising of all the pueblos against
Spain. The twenty-five villages of the four language families had
never been united before and he had suspicion and lethargy to overcome. Executive drive like his is not usual in the pueblos, where
modesty and communal action is the law; but Popé, says tradition,
was a medicine man who had been with the Apache and learned
procedures unknown to pueblo people.

He used shrewd planning for he did not try to rouse his own people
first but went to Taos, of the Tigua, where several rebellions had
already been started. Taos was slow to convince, but legend says that
he took the important men into the kiva and showed them three
shining messengers, his supernatural helpers.

"Devils" the Spaniards called those messengers when they heard
the story afterward. They questioned and questioned the prisoners
whom they took, searching to find out what could possibly have made

...they had kept their ancient ceremonies....

. . . .the whole town may turn out in its ancient dress. . . .

such prosperous villagers rebel. They heard that Popé had promised "that they would be living according to the laws of their ancestors", laws made to satisfy the powers of earth and rain. Their fulfilment meant that the Indians would of couse "harvest great quantities of corn and beans, large bales of cotton, pumpkins and very large melons and cantaloupe and with these they could fill their houses. They would be full of health and rest".

Taos was convinced and, after Taos, the other Pueblos. One day in 1680 there went out through pueblo country a knotted cord showing the number of days which were to pass before the rebellion broke. It was carried from pueblo to pueblo by the war captains and with a threat, said some of the prisoners afterward, that those who did not join the revolt would be killed themselves. Longing for the old ways had eaten its way deep into the whole country. Even the Hopi sent up signal fires of acquiescence.

The rebellion had to explode too soon, but it exploded. Beginning at Tesuque of the Tewa, churches and records went up in flames; Spaniards were killed if they did not get away. Horrified, the governor reported that the once model converts, "carried away by their anger and hate of the Holy Faith, broke into pieces and burned the divine images of Jesus Christ and the Virgin Mary and those of all the saints and things pertaining to the Divine Cult, without leaving a single cross or sign of Christianity ever having been there".

The Tewa had in the midst of their country the Spanish capital of Santa Fe, and they marched on it. Refugees from all over the country had gathered in its adobe fortress where the governor had his

117

cannon, but he had forgotten about supplies. Surely there was no danger of a siege from such tractable, unorganized people as these Indians, many of whom had once been officers' servants! The Indians sent a messenger to the fortress with two crosses: a red one for war and a white one for peace. Naturally the governor chose war, for "we must make them to respect the mandates of His Majesty". He tried to stimulate such respect by executing under the eyes of the besiegers, forty-seven Indian prisoners. The Indians watched but did not move. In a week the governor's water and food were gone. He and the soldiers and civilians of Santa Fe marched out of the garrison and to the south, the Indians still watching.

Then came the twelve years which should have been glorious for the Indians, if the chances had not been all against them. They had wanted so little—only corn, beans and squash and peace in their ancient life. But they could not have peace, even though they did as Popé exhorted them and discarded their Spanish clothes and Spanish seeds and their wives, married in the Spanish church. For the Spanish army kept creeping out from El Paso in Texas where it had taken refuge, and the villagers had to perch in mountain strongholds, stealing down now and then to get a little food. And the food failed them. Instead of the great crops promised by Popé's messengers, there came a drought which might almost have been sent by an avenging God. Village after village was starving.

From his refuge at El Paso del Norte, the Pass of the North, Governor Otermin made the move which really ended the rebellion: he confirmed to the Pueblos the right to their land. They accepted.

Land and corn was the basis of their life, and if they could have this one thing they were willing to give up even peace in their ancient ways, practising them, henceforth, in unpeaceful secrecy. His Majesty's government signed grants of five, six, and seven miles square for every pueblo but Hopi and Zuni which were so surrounded by empty spaces that a land grant seemed an absurdity.

Then a new governor was appointed and at last, after twelve years, De Vargas rode in triumph through Santa Fe. He had been having his troubles, rounding up the Pueblos for the sake of their souls, and some of the Tewa had been long on Potrero Viejo, refusing to come down. The San Ildefonso, says the legend, had remained on Black Mesa, fooling the Spaniards by throwing down reeds from the top, as though they had a spring up there that would keep them alive. In the end they all gave in and Spanish rule seemed there to stay.

This was the very time that the great colonial machine was weakening. Church and state were no longer pulling together. Priests had no government supplies for feeding their converts; converts became insolent to priests; soldiers failed to help tame them. The three-part system of missionary, military, and civilian estate owner was ceasing to function.

Worse than that, the fierce nomads, on horses stolen from the Spaniards themselves, were cutting off one village after another from the long Rio Grande chain. Some had faded out during the rebellion, some had moved away out of pure fear as the dreadful circle of Ute, Kiowa, Comanche and Apache closed closer around them. Even before the rebellion, cries had gone up to the garrison as one town after another went under, beginning toward Texas and working north, but often the town was left, church and all, and the inhabitants moved down toward El Paso or out toward the Hopi.

The Spaniards kept sending out squads of soldiers to gallop hopelessly through the wilderness after a homeless enemy fleeter than they were. The governor paid bounties for the ears of Apache and Navajo brought to his palace at Santa Fe. The Piro villages had disappeared, the Tigua were reduced from the great nation reported by first explorers to a few towns with wide, empty spaces in between. The numbers of Tewa dwindled in their villages. They had to keep peace with the Spaniards now and the Spaniards with them. The land was all important, and conquered and conquerors clung together trying to hold it.

This was the time when Spanish farmers began to move in among the Tewa. Spain had forbidden the Indians to alienate their lands, but there were empty spaces now which seemed as though they would never be populated again, and the grants which had to be made to Spanish citizens kept overlapping with Indian property. There must have been mixture in those days and the quiet readjustment which comes neither from law nor schooling but from neighborly living. When the Tewa became Mexican citizens, they were living very much like the Spanish settlers who helped to populate their villages. Like them they voted and sat on juries. Then their ways parted.

In 1848 New Mexico became a territory of the United States, and in 1850 that territory legislated that the Indians were not citizens. In 1910 the Federal Government decreed that they were wards and need not pay taxes. From that time they became more Indian, setting themselves off against two groups of Whites, the Spanish Americans and the citizens of the United States, but the Tewa had had centuries of white companionship. Theirs could be no aloofness like that of the Hopi, while their villages clustered around Santa Fe and travelers and pedlars stopped constantly at their doors. Even with no intermarriage there was a sharing of customs so that a pueblo could maintain its separateness only by the sternest internal rules. Many of them made such rules and it is in pursuance of those that Whites are shut out on certain days of the year. "Probably something shocking", concluded the first agents, little realizing that secrecy was the only protection left for Tewa integrity.

Then cities grew up and the nearby Tewa became the obvious symbol for Indian art and picturesqueness. For forty or fifty years white Americans have been going to Tewa dances. For the last ten or fifteen years artists have been making them famous. The Tewa cannot remain or become old style Indians. The artistic signs on the highway which point the way to their pleasant villages are guide to thousands of cars in a year. The villages themselves, clustering under the trees near a church, have stores, gasoline stations, an occasional sun porch or a bathroom. What has happened to the old ways whose expression was traded so long ago for land? Those ways persist, for the human race is finding out that customs so sacred can never be eradicated, only changed slowly into something else.

The Tewa keep their old form of government which only now shows signs of lapsing, after running along for three hundred years,

121

parallel with the governors and lieutenants imposed by the Spanish. It is a government very different from that of Hopi and Zuni. Its essence is the division of the whole population into halves. Winter and Summer people they are called, and each has its kiva and each its priestly ruler, the cacique, who takes full charge of the town for half the year. Toward spring the Winter man gives the people over to the Summer man, and toward autumn the Summer man gives them back. Each leader while he is in office must attend to all the ceremonies and must pray for the good of the village. He has his job for life, though he only works six months out of every year. The right hand man and the left hand man, who assist him, move up in order to take his place, so that there is always an assistant in training. As for the governor and the assistant officers, the caciques appoint them.

It is an interesting form of two-party system, where the membership of the parties is hereditary, not optional. One belongs to the same half as his father. It is plain that, if one half should weaken or die out, the nicely balanced system of government would be thrown out of gear. The Tewa villages are having their troubles with that problem. In some, one cacique or the other is now missing: in some, one-half has attained unusual power. The voices of progressives and conservatives are heard mixed with those of Summer and Winter until the people can no longer be handed over as a whole from one season to the other. Santa Clara, the pueblo which developed the greatest number of factions, has found it simpler to reorganize under a new United States law which allows Indian communities to hold land in common under a charter; but Nambe, having been without caciques for some years, appointed new ones and went back to the old plan.

While this old government has been slowly adjusting itself to the needs of people who care little about Summer and Winter but much about progress and conservatism, the old religious dances have still been going on. The most important of them are secret and no White may go to see the masked kachinas or accompany pilgrims to the hills, but the Tewa have fused the religion of Dios and that of the corn, or perhaps the early missionaries showed them how. Every pueblo has a patron saint and no one but the Tewa themselves remember that there are Indian names for such towns as San Juan, Santa Clara and San Ildefonso.

On the saint's day the wagons and automobiles gather from Spanish and Indian dwellings, all the way up and down the river valley. The church is crowded. The kneeling figures, all dark haired and dark eyed show, now the high, beaked nose and bloodless skin that proclaims Spanish ancestry, now the smooth, broad features of the Indian, tinted golden brown. Glancing along a row of bowed heads you may see, first the traditional black Mantilla of the Spanish woman; then the flowered shawl adopted by her sister of the pueblos and next the small hat and permanently waved hair worn by the daughters of both. "Dominus vobiscum", says the padre and all the voices, Indian and white, murmur together: "Et con spiritu tuo". The little organ quavers a Latin hymn. The Indian acolyte, in bright kerchief and tightly wrapped blanket, genuflects before the altar decked with paper roses.

123

Mass is over and the worshippers patter and tramp into the plaza, in cowboy boots, mocassins or high heeled slippers. No one goes home, for now that the Christian God has been honored, the gods of the pueblos have their turn. If it is in summer, *the whole town may turn out in its ancient dress*, the men in embroidered kilt, streaming hair, dangling fox skin and turquoise jewelry: the women in black *manta*, their heads surmounted with the lofty structure, painted with turquoise and orange and tipped with feathers, which represents the clouds. This is the corn dance, done upon a day in summer which falls on the name day of some saint, chosen by the wise Franciscans, *a day on which the whole village is graciously open to guests of all kinds*.

They crowd into the adobe houses where modern chairs are arranged primly around the sitting room, beneath the colored calendars and the saints' pictures which hang on the walls. In one corner may stand a huge brass bed and in another a phonograph — even a radio. If this is a modern house, like some in San Juan, there may be a table with embroidered cover and an electric light with fancy shade. In the kitchen, the enormous kettles are bubbling full of beans, chili and stew while the hostess in her white buckskin boots pads to and fro all the afternoon feeding relays of silent, smiling visitors.

Corn dances are summer ceremonies but if you go to the pueblos in winter, when hunting days used to begin, you may see the stately deer, the huge headed buffalo and the little, skipping fawns prancing in the plaza, decked with horns and spruces boughs. Again, it is the eagle dance, when two great human birds, with yellow painted feet

124

. . . . a day on which the whole village is open. . . .

. . . . to guests of all kinds.

If it is the modern San Ildefonso you see.... shops of pottery makers.

and sweeping wings, circle and swoop to the sound of singing. There is a measured dignity about all the dances whose steady rhythm changes so subtly that you must watch closely to notice it. The clear colors of white, yellow and turquoise, the flowing hair, the one spot of red on the cheek, are beautiful to European as well as to Indian eyes. But there is little European flavor about the clowns with their bodies striped grimly in black and gray, their grinning faces topped with withered corn husks. These are beings so powerful that they may make fun even of sacred things and so, with solemn thoroughness, they caricature the Navajo fire dance, the Apache "devil dance", the Tewa deer dance — and the Christian mass. The spectators, Navajo, Apache and White, roar with laughter. During those few hours, they have entered with the clowns into a country beyond good and evil, they are having a holiday from all rules.

Wandering through the plaza after the dance, you see a town which looks like any pleasant Spanish American village. *If it is the modern San Ildefonso, you see the* artistic signs of painters and *shops of pottery makers.* If it is Santa Clara or San Juan, the shining racks of ebony-bright black pottery may be spread out on the ground for sale.

They are not the pots of ancient days, or at least not many of them. These villages have found the shapes which appeal to the Whites, not for carrying water or storing beans, but for perfectly designed ornament in a modernistic room. Why not? A beautiful pot is an expensive article, judged by the cost of time and labor in the modern world, and pueblo people, who are not rich, cannot afford such things for their own use. It pays them to buy their household goods at the

← Maria Martinez of San Ildefonso used to bring her pots to Santa Fe....

ten cent store and to sell their pots as Cape Cod farmers used to sell their heirlooms. In this age handmade articles are for the rich.

The start in commercial pottery came about 1915 at San Ildefonso. The village had always been making pottery, like all the others, and even through Spanish days its women continued to shape their storage jars and mixing bowls of cream, red, and black clay. They had another type which belonged specially to the Tewa pueblos and which must have come down from very ancient times. It was deep black, made by smothering the flame in which a red painted pot is fired so that the soot becomes ingrained in its sides. When those sides are polished for hours with a smooth pebble after the pueblo manner, there results an inimitable, gleaming ebony. If the fire is not smothered, the pot is mahogany red.

Maria Martinez of San Ildefonso used to bring her pots to the experts at *Santa Fe* where students were eager to have the old art continued. Once she brought a polished black pot with geometric figures in dull black. It was unlike anything ever done in the pueblos and she was urged to make more. Since that time Maria and her husband, Julian, have become world famous for their striking jars and bowls, hand-polished to mechanical perfection, decorated with the classic restraint of angular masses or the flowing curves of the water serpent, a figure in pueblo ceremonies.

These decorations are the work of Julian Martinez, perhaps the first pueblo man ever to engage in pottery making. It was a woman's art in old days, and all the designs came from a woman's brain and experience. Why should the men not enter the commercial world by

126

this gateway as by any other, bringing a different training and new ideas? Several men at San Ildefonso have accepted this possibility, but that is not the end of the changes brought about by commercial pottery. When Maria and Julian Martinez had become justly famous, every visitor who bought a pot wished to see their names scratched on its base. They could not produce enough and had to have help. It is the well-known step with which every white business man is familiar, as the little one man shop expands into the large one. Until now it had never happened in the pueblos. From time immemorial the women who made a pot had dug her clay, mixed it, coiled it, polished, painted and fired. She was not an artist any more than a clay digger, for the process was all one. Now the stages are separated. The shaping of the pot and the painting are done respectively by Maria and Julian, while all the unskilled processes are delegated to paid helpers. It is the beginning of a small factory, just as such things began in the Middle Ages.

It was sheer economic luck that an ancient shape, color and design of the Tewa struck the right note for modern white taste, for many Indian products, striking though they are, require a special house to show them off. Santa Clara and San Juan have followed San Ildefonso's economic lead, but the ancient separateness of the pueblos still holds good, and each has its own kind of black and red ware. Little Tesuque failed of economic luck for her ancient designs of thin black scrolls on white looked neither strange nor striking. What is such a pueblo to do?—invent something fantastic which will sell as "Indian", or stick with classic devotion to the ancient style, too expensive for home use, too inconspicuous to sell. This is one of the problems occupying the friends of Indian art, among them the new Crafts Board of the Indian Office.

The quaint shop signs, which dot the more modern pueblos, advertise not only pottery but painting. Within the present generation there has dawned on the white world the realization that Indians, their picture sense unwarped by floods of baby picture books and colored advertisements, can paint the scenes of their own native life with a purity of color and jewel-like detail which calls to mind ancient work by the Chinese or the Persians. Indians had never painted on paper before: they had never indulged in art for art's sake, but now that domestic articles can be bought more cheaply than made, their sense of decoration has found a new outlet. "Before art came into existence", said one of the pupils at the Santa Fe school, "the principal of native products of the soil were beans, corn, squashes and pinyon nuts. The introduction of art work greatly changed their daily activities. In fact, it changed farmers into artists." Some of the pueblos object, and rightly, to the portraying of their sacred dances to which Whites are not admitted. The classically beautiful public dances of the Tewa provide enough material for any artists, and many, like Abel Sanchez, are already famous. Many an artist chooses as subjects dances, not from his own pueblo, but rather those from alien pueblos, thus preserving the sanctity of his own and particularly, his place among his own people.

The farmers have not all turned artists. The concern of the Tewa is still most of all with their land—that river land which has shaped their history. It caused them to accept the Spaniards rather than give it up; it caused them to adopt the weapon of secrecy because, in such desirable country, they could not have isolation; it is now causing changes in farming methods which may revolutionize their ancient cycle. For a while at the beginning of this century that land seemed to be disappearing. Since early Spanish days white settlers had been moving into Tewa land, often with a government grant, and for years the "neighbors" had been living peacefully among the Tewa while the two peoples grew together in general customs. Then the white Americans moved in, surrounding them both, and if they did not take land they took water. It was considered perfectly ethical in pioneer days for a man to tap a stream at any point and remove as much water as he wanted, without thinking of those further down. Tesuque and Nambe lost almost all their water and the other villages much. In 1932 when a government land board investigated the situation, it found that, not only was the water going but the Tewa, in one way or another, had lost over four hundred thousand dollars worth of land.

The same thing had happened with the other pueblos, though not on such a large scale. In fact 20,000 acres all together were gone. The government, which had promised to take care of its wards in this respect, has been occupied ever since in settling claims, buying back land, or paying the Pueblos in money. Those payments have meant one of the greatest jumps ever taken by the Pueblos from the ancient to the modern world. They were not made to individuals, for individuals did not own pueblo land, but merely used it with the consent of the village. The village received the payment and spent it, like a highly capitalized modern farming company, for new ditches and up-to-date machinery. No amount of instruction would have produced the same result.

Land is likely to influence the future of the Tewa to a much further extent, for the valley of the Great River is still the garden spot of New Mexico and New Mexico is filling up. Where the methods of irrigation taught by the Spanish fathers used to do well enough, now eager farmers count every drop of leakage from the old earthern dams. No one in the valley can any longer practise wasteful irrigation for any reason whatever. A conservancy board has investigated and revised the whole plan of ditching; soil conservation experts have reported on the use of the range; agriculturists have demonstrated the best paying crops for the space. If the Tewa long still for corn, beans and squash, a law above that of the white man decrees that sometimes alfalfa or market produce is more economical. They have united their fate with that of the river valley; they must change as it changes.

6

Taos by the Buffalo Country

The Pueblo plateau breaks at the east into a tangle of mountains, walling it from the Great Plains. In former days that mountain wall was the barrier between the farmer Indians and the hunters. To the west of it was corn country where every stream and seepage of water had at some time its patiently cultivated plants and its cluster of dwellings. Because of the corn, people could settle and, because they were settled, they could weave cotton, paint delicate pottery, and gather month after month for ceremonies. To the east of the mountain wall was buffalo country where men could have plenty of food and an exciting life without settling down. Over its wide cloud-shadowed spaces, between the trickling sandy rivers, roamed the Apache, Arapaho, Cheyenne, Kiowa, and Comanche, clothed in

131

skins, eating buffalo meat, living in tipis of buffalo hide which might be pitched anywhere between Colorado and Mexico.

Just beneath the mountain wall at the very edge of Pueblo country *perches Taos.* Far below it lies the valley of the Rio Grande with the other farmer villages; above it a narrow pass leads to the Plains. In ancient days wild Apache and Comanche used to come through that pass, sometimes to fight, sometimes to trade buffalo for beans, corn and buckskin and to leap with the home-staying Indians in war dances, very different from the sedate pacing of the rain makers. Through that gap also, the Taos used to sally forth to hunt buffalo, to fight the Utes, and to escape from the Spaniards.

This doorway to the Plains has influenced all of Taos life. In this pueblo you find shields of buffalo skin; moccasins with hard soles, fringed leggings, tall, blanketed figures with braided hair. It is the costume and the aspect of the Plains Indians, and one thinks of those wild warriors on seeing the hawk nose and high cheek bones which show beneath the swathing blanket of a Taos man. The blanket however is of white cotton such as was once woven in the pueblos though now it is bought in a store and the figure is slenderer and smaller than that of a typical "buffalo Indian". Here is a mixture of customs and, perhaps, of blood. Like all mixtures of good ingredients, it means stimulus and new possibilities for old material.

White people find something akin to themselves in the spirit of Taos. Picturesque and ancient as it seems, secretive and aloof beyond any other pueblo save Santo Domingo of the Keres, Taos has an attitude that smacks of our own puritanism. Not that it forbids dancing

Just beneath the mountain wall....perches Taos.

or color or music or even, in ancient days, the keeping of several wives. These are externals, important to one group of Puritans, unimportant to the next. The Puritan essential is conscience, duty, and an unbending application of the law whatever it may be. Some of the other pueblos find it hard to state their law; their people simply move along together in neighborly contentment—or such is their ideal. But the laws of Taos are rigid. Beneath the beautifully patterned ceremonies is a sternness foreign to many pueblos but familiar to those two groups of outsiders, the Whites and the Plains Indians.

You drive to Taos from Santa Fe up the winding curves of the gorge which once formed the first lap of the Santa Fe trail east. Here is no more flat, desert scenery, all purple and rose emptiness under a blue sky. The Rio Grande flows between rocky walls topped with evergreens; a cold breeze blows down through the gorge and, in the green coves by the river, apples grow like those of New England. You mount the last steep pitch in the sudden chill of mountain wind and before you stretches a green plateau backed by hills. Taos Peak, Flute Mountain, Bluebird Tail and Bow Mountain raise their tree covered slopes, cloud-shadowed in summer, snow-capped in winter, as the eastern wall of the pueblo world.

Yet Taos at its gateway looks more like a pueblo of ancient times than any now occupied. On both sides of a little river terraced houses are banked up to four and five storeys. Only in the last few years have there been painted window frames with glass, for these were not allowed in the village except in the church which has a "different religion". On ground and terraces great stacks of firewood from the

133

←— *Each has its own kivas....*

mountains are heaped, for Taos is cold in winter. Beside them stand drying-racks for meat and in front of each house a beehive shaped oven. Spain herself has forgotten these ovens made of adobe by her first settlers, but the Pueblos learned of them and use them still.

Organization is apparent in this pueblo even at first sight. It does not straggle but is built in two compact masses, one on the north of the river, one on the south. *Each has its own kivas*, each has its place in ceremonies. Around the town is an adobe wall, and you soon learn that this wall marks a definite boundary. Inside it no stranger may visit without a permit from the governor; there may be no separate houses; no villager may cut his hair or go without his blanket.

This is a village conscious of itself and not maintaining old standards simply because new ones have not reached it. Taos, used to being looked at and discussed, is maintaining the old ways knowingly and of set purpose. Even more tenaciously than the Keres, the village keeps to its old form of housebuilding, its old costume, its old religion. "Our ways would lose their power if they were changed," say the Taos, and those who study history understand. The automobile has changed the attitude of the United States toward church going. Even the slightest material innovation might threaten the religion of Taos.

It is a religion which points back to the beginning of the world like that of the other pueblos. The Taos came, they say, not from the dark womb of Mother Earth but from a lake, far in the north. They wandered south and met people who "taught them how to live". Then they went farther south and finally north again camping at many places. The last part of the legend is attested by the ruins on their own plateau. Finally they came to that place which the white men call Taos and they call, the Place of Red Willows, for they are Red Willow People.

Taos speaks the language of the Tigua or Tiwa, a once widespread tongue which was related to the Tewa as German, say, is related to English. When written history dawned upon the pueblo with the Spanish accounts, it was more or less where it is now. In the wide Rio Grande valley below it were some twelve to sixteen sister villages of the so-called province of "Tiguex", some by the river, some pushing east toward the Plains. Prosperous villages they must have been, for the one which has been unearthed shows huge kivas with mural decorations such as are found nowhere else, but wild Apaches on one side and civilized Spaniards on the other proved their undoing. Now there are left only Taos at the north with its tiny mountain neighbor, Picuris, and a hundred miles to the south, Sandia and Isleta, indistinguishable in many ways from the Spanish American towns of the great river valley.

Taos of the Red Willow People looked in Spanish days as much like a fortress as a town. Four and five storeys high it stood as it does today, but without a door in its thick adobe walls. Light came through the tiny windows and the entrance was through a hatchway in the roof, reached by a ladder which was no more than a notched pine log. When signal fires above the pass to the Plains showed that enemies were coming, the ladders were pulled in, and the two banks of houses on the sides of the stream formed two forts impregnable to arrows, where all the villagers could gather.

They gathered often in ancient times when the Navajo swept in from the east, the Ute from the north, or the Apache from the west. Navajo were the worst enemies and any scalp was called "a Navajo", but the Taos did not fight all the wanderers as the other Pueblo people did. They were too close to make that advisable. Besides, they wanted to hunt the buffalo themselves, so they had a sort of shaky alliance with the Apache, some of whom even settled on the plateau when the domestic life looked good to them. The Comanche, though they once besieged the Taos in their fort and lost some forty-nine men as a result, were generally friends. It was they who taught the Red Willow people the war dances which lately have spread like wildfire through the pueblos. Taos used to hold a great fair after harvest when all these wanderers came bringing buffalo meat and hides, and got in exchange Taos corn and beans and dressed white buckskin. The next summer when the grass had come up and the buffalo were oaming on the flat plains which are now eastern New Mexico and Colorado, the Taos men would sally forth to camp near the Apache and come back laden with jerked meat, hides for their shields, moccasins, and great horned heads for their buffalo dance.

While the Spaniards slowly mastered the valley of the Rio Grande and while the Apache surged along their borders, cutting off one outlying village after another, Taos perched in peace among the mountains. One of Coronado's scouting parties visited it and reported in wonder about the fortified town with its fifteen thousand souls. But Taos on the east, like Hopi on the west, was one of the lucky pueblos not immediately worth conquering.

136

As the years rolled by and Spanish civilization stretched further and further up the Rio Grande valley, isolation diminished. Taos was baptised. Taos secured a governor and a set of officers like the other "reduced" towns. The extra officers were a sort of consulate to take care of the tiresome business of dealing with Whites. They dealt with the Spaniards and allowed them to ride up through the pass hunting for Apache—even helped them in fact. For a time the little fortified village and the soldiers of Spain had an unofficial fighting alliance.

Then the Spanish grants came closer and closer to Taos. Now there are white people living on its own high plateau and there is a church for Whites and Indians. The Taos rose up one day and killed the priest and his Spanish guards, but it did no good. Finally the village began to get uneasy. Its fighters and buffalo hunters had not expected to be dragging stones for a new church or meeting at sunrise to sing matins. They were outraged when the priest intruded upon their family affairs by objecting to more than one wife. They met in the kivas and talked over ways of putting a stop to the invasion. Then they took a piece of buckskin, sign of a hunting people, and painted it with symbols which were an invitation to rebellion. It was sent to the other pueblos, all down the Rio Grande and across the desert. Most of them agreed, but the peaceful Hopi, the last people at the western edge, did not. They were too far away to see the need for fighting. Four more such leagues were started before the last one, led by Popé of San Juan.

Indian power lasted twelve years as we have told. After the Spaniards had granted the Pueblos land, De Vargas, the new governor, moved from one to another urging people to come down from their rocky refuges and go to work. Most of them received him joyfully, so he says, and indeed, they must have been hungry, but some of the Keres and Tewa were still perched on their mesas and, as for Taos and Picuris, they had disappeared. They were camped with some Tewa in the pass beyond Taos and when asked "to come down to their villages like humble vassals (as they are) of his Majesty" they said "they did not want peace but war." They got it. De Vargas sacked the town; blackened places seem to show that he burned it. The Indians fled to caves where they kept themselves alive on their bean harvest, but the Spaniards followed and took the beans. Only then did the Indians come down.

De Vargas put up a new church for them and instructed them that, until a priest could come, they must say prayers for themselves at morning, evening and midday. They said they would. Then they requested their "father" to "retire and leave them the freedom of their village, in order that their fields might not be utterly consumed". He did so after embracing them, and Taos made an effort to live submissively. It came so hard that five priests and twenty Spaniards more were killed in the next few years. Then the worst rebels from Taos and Picuris gave up. They picked up their goods and marched out of the pass to live on the Plains with the Apache. A long, weary journey De Vargas' men had, off into Oklahoma looking for them in the cold, but did not find them. That particular group of Pueblo Indians went permanently wild.

The rest settled down. They had Spanish officers whom they

installed once a year by handing out the canes of office as they do still. They had a priest whom they supported with armfuls of corn and wood. Around them on the plateau three or four Spanish villages shared the runlets of water from their mountains. "Neighbors" the Taos called them and they lived with them peaceably, though they did once ask them kindly to move a league away from the pueblo. In 1793 Don Fernando Chacon, the governor at Santa Fe, made a grant of land overlapping the Taos grant. That was the beginning of "old Touse" on the Santa Fe trail, headquarters of trappers and Mountain Men, which became an American settlement while Santa Fe was still Spanish.

A sophisticated artists' town is Fernando de Taos at present, with its pastel colored adobe houses whose bulging walls look as if they were made of melting sugar. What was once a frontier post, changed imperceptibly to Mexican during the Spanish rule in the Southwest, then settlers of the United States began to nose their way across the Plains. Out in the buffalo country traders were setting up their log forts by the shallow, treacherous rivers. Trappers were scouting down one stream and up the next toward the distant, western mountains and one of the few openings which would let them through was the pass above Taos. The Plainsmen who reached the pueblo by that route were almost Plains Indians when they arrived, dressed in buckskin, living on pemmican and followed by an Indian wife or two. After them came the first mule trains of the Santa Fe trail.

It was a two months' journey in those days from Independence, Kansas, to Santa Fe. Along the Arkansas River went the trotting

139

caravans, past Bent's log fort where spent and hungry men came to exchange their last possessions for horses and food, up over the "Rat" pass of the Sangre de Cristo to the little Mexican town of Fernando de Taos. The Spanish province of New Mexico put up a custom house there and winked, for a price, at all sorts of contraband which could never have passed the big Mexican cities. Five hundred dollars per wagonload would get almost anything in and you could leave half your wagons hidden outside the town and pile all the goods on the rest. Taos Indian acted as guides and scouts for the caravans. They knew the tricks of the Apache who were the pest of the traders and they kept a lookout on the mountain top to give smoke signals when the road was clear. They came to have friends among the Whites as few other pueblos did. Kit Carson lived for fifteen years at "old Touse", and Charles Bent even longer. Pattie and the St. Vrains used to come and go, sleeping on the floors of its adobe houses. Meantime the United States, whose organized existence they had almost forgotten, declared war on Mexico and before any one knew much of what was happening, General Kearney was in Santa Fe. The pueblos were under American rule.

Taos awoke to find that its American neighbor, Charles Bent, was military governor of New Mexico. That meant little to the Indians but much to the Spanish farmers, their neighbors on the plateau. These Spaniards thought that Mexico had been too hasty in giving in and they wanted to fight. They urged the Indians to help them, telling of atrocities, and promising plunder. The Taos did not like to think about any new oppression so they rose on the day the Spaniards had

140

. . . . *mother and child* . . . . ⟶

. . . . *clothespins swinging against a puffy sky beside oldtime ladders over new window frames with glass.*

— *She follows her mother to the great hive-shaped oven which stands outside the house. . . .*

set. Even when most of the Spaniards dropped out they went ahead. They hunted Americans through the streets of Touse, they broke into Governor Bent's house, scalped him alive and killed him.

The Cheyenne, out on the Plains, heard about the tragedy and wanted to avenge their friend, Charles Bent, but the white soldiers preferred to do it themselves. It took them a day or two to surround the Indians in their Spanish church and to batter down its walls. One shot, say the Taos, got lost in the belfry and went zooming around and around like a great beetle. They saved the statue of the blessed Virgin from the church though she was "all of a sweat" from fear. One hundred fifty Taos were killed. Then men and women came out with white flags and crucifixes, and on their knees, begged for peace. They had to surrender the war chief and six others to hanging, but the war chief deliberately tried to break jail and was shot.

Quiet again. Now wagons rolled over the Santa Fe trail but since New Mexico was all American ground, they did not bother to come up through the mountains to Taos. Their drivers foregathered at the saloons and *bailes* of Santa Fe and once again Taos was at peace.

It has been at peace ever since. The ancient terraced village, though it looks like a museum piece for the archaeologists, is a prosperous farming community with modern ditches, fenced fields, tractors, threshers and a herd of fine cattle. There has been government help in getting these things but there has also been the cooperation of Taos. Taos farmers are shrewd and able and, though they wish to keep their religion, they also wish to earn a living just as they always did. Once it was hunting and corn, now it is cows and alfalfa.

141

On the hill beyond the village stands the brand new hospital and the government school, where a child may learn how to make a dress, buy a railroad ticket, mend a wagon and to read, write and figure. All children go to school with permission of the pueblo but with reservations. When a bus load of children was being brought back from the higher school at Santa Fe, the pueblo asked that they might wait, because of an eclipse which would bring bad luck. The government bus waited. When once a year it becomes the turn of certain boys to be initiated for many months into the secrets of the village, the school excuses them. Outside the pueblo English, automobiles, and the comic strip; within, the old ways that give power!

After a Taos child has been presented to the sun his mother lays an ear of corn beside her baby to keep him safe and gives him an elk tooth to suck so his own teeth will come quickly. When it is time for him to talk, she holds him in her lap while she squats beside the fire parching corn. No sooner are the corn kernels in the pan over the fire than they begin jumping and popping, all of them noisy together. So she wants her baby's words to come out, falling over each other in their haste.

Juniper wood from the mountains crackles in the corner fireplace, for the Taos object to stoves. They object to beds also, and the blankets, Navajo, Hopi or machine made, from the trader's store are rolled in a corner. Perhaps linoleum covers the earthern floor and a bright saint's picture hangs on the wall. Or there may be a drum with painted sides, a flute, or a bunch of parrot feathers for the ceremonial dances.

The mother pads about the house in her great white buckskin boots, their wide legs folded in tiers like the leggings of the roving Apache or the boots of Spanish cavaliers. She wears a long calico dress, belted with a handwoven sash bought from the Hopi. Her long hair is tied at the back of her neck and banged in front, just above her black eyebrows. The child's father stamps in and out of the house, a farmer in blue jeans and sheepskin coat; he would once have worn shirt and leggings of fringed buckskin. Two braids hang beside his face as they would have hung in old times and over his modern clothes, he wraps a blanket. He never wears shoes with heels inside the village and, if he owns a cowboy hat, he leaves it outside.

It is a close little family, not like the large ones of Hopi and Zuni, where the nearby houses are crowded with uncles and aunts and a child's first years are full of learning about relatives and clans and his duties toward them. Here, at the edge of the pueblo world, the family is small again and white people find it easy to understand the little group of father, *mother* and *children*. They understand, too, the ambition and independence that make a Taos Indian as much like a warrior of the Plains as like the gentle and communally minded Pueblo people.

In childhood the boy runs about the pueblo, staring with dark, unrevealing eyes at the chattering tourists and asking them for pennies, since that is what tourists are good for. Growing older, he follows his father to the fields, where he learns to hoe and irrigate. He hears the ditch boss call out from the housetops when the men must gather for ditch cleaning just as they used to gather for hunting and for war. He learns that every citizen must do his share of the work or pay

143

a fine, for so Taos manages its business. He and his father must take their turn in keeping the cattle from the cornfields, as men did long ago when they guarded the horses on a trip to the buffalo Plains.

The girl stays in the house. If Taos were really in the buffalo country, she would make the garden and tan the skins while her men were fighting and hunting, but Taos is like the pueblos in its treatment of women. The girl brings water from the stream which supplies the household and which, though it runs through the middle of the village, is kept clean by unwritten ordinance. *She follows her mother to the great hive-shaped oven which stands outside the house,* tall as the child herself, and as large inside as a dog kennel. It is only a single chamber with no place for a fire under it. The fire is made in the oven itself and when the adobe walls have absorbed a deal of the heat, the embers are raked out and the solid, round loaves of unleavened corn or wheat bread are shoved in on a wooden paddle. Then the oven is closed with a stone or a plank or a sheet of galvanized iron, according to the modernity of the cook and there ensues a slow, mild baking which even the modern textbooks recommend. It was the way in which beans were cooked in the cupboard beside a colonial fireplace. It was the method of seventeenth century Spain and it survives in the pueblos.

The girl's mother has probably made that oven herself just as she has the corner fireplace in her one or two room dwelling. She renews them every year for adobe, while easy to build up, crumbles easily and a pueblo woman must constantly plaster. Her special bout of it, which corresponds to a white woman's spring cleaning, is just before

Saint Geronimo's day on September twenty-ninth. Then each woman plasters her whole house, white within and smooth brown without, until the whole pueblo looks like a house model on exhibition.

Plastering and cooking are her main crafts. She does not make baskets and no one remembers that she ever did. Her grandmothers made painted pots, so the scrap heaps indicate, but now her pots are of uncolored clay, more like the crude utensils of the Plains than the delicate, artistic ware of the Pueblos. She does a little beadwork now because the schools have taught it but beadwork was not an old art of Taos. In fact, the Taos woman is not the independent property owner and craftswoman of the western pueblos. In her we come much nearer the dependent helpmeet of white tradition.

Out of her adobe doorway, when her children are five or six, she sends them to school, for Taos has doorways now instead of the old hatchways in the roofs through which the ladders were pulled in every night. Taos like other pueblos has a new school, with hardwood floors and shining windows, with shops, stoves and sewing machines.

The children learn to answer to American as well as to Indian names and presently, they find that they have Spanish names too. For the Taos were baptised long ago with the appellations of the conquerors, famous names like Roybal, Mirabal and Lujan, which are still carried on the church books. The child was brought to the baptismal font soon after he was presented to the sun and when he goes to school, he goes to mass. Not every Sunday, for the priest has to cover all the little Spanish towns on the Taos plateau, but once a month, the boy kneels in the little whitewashed church which replaced

145

the old one, battered down by United States troops. He hears mass in Latin and, perhaps a little sermon in Spanish; he learns the names of the saints and knows that on their days some of the most exciting fiestas known to Taos occur.

There is Saint Anthony's day, when people dance outside the houses of all the Tonys and Tonitas in the village, and San Isidro's day, when the image of the farmer saint is carried through the fields as it used to be in mediaeval Spain. There is St. John's day in mid-summer, when all over the Southwest, roosters are buried in the earth and pulled out by galloping horsemen, but Christmas is the best. Most pueblos honor Dios and his saints at this holiest time by performing their own native dances in church as the priests long ago encouraged them to do. It was the best way to bring them to the true religion step by step, thought those wise men. On Christmas they sometimes add old Spanish and Moorish mummers' masques straight from the seventeenth century.

But Taos outdoes itself. The Blessed Virgin and the saints could not but rejoice to see children dance before the church on the eve of the birth of Christ and to be carried in procession themselves around the holiday village. It is like a peasant fiesta in old Spain when men and maidens carry the holy images and youths discharge shotguns and bonfires blaze all the way to the church to light the Christchild. For two days people dance throughout the village, as the priests once directed them to welcome Our Lord. Then comes the white man's New Year, when the governor and his aides are installed and an oath is administered by a notary public. (No other pueblo goes as white as this.)

146

This is the quiet season of the old Taos religion, which demands that the earth lie still at germinating time, that no wood be chopped, no wagons roll and no trade be consummated. Mother Earth and Mother of God are revered together and as a climax, comes either the dance of the buffalo or of those Spanish religious mummers called "matachines."

There is nothing inconsistent to Taos people in this fusion of two religions. The "altar house" and its predecessors have nearly three hundred years of service behind them and theirs is the only white priest officiating within the pueblo walls. Perhaps the Taos, who crowd the church on feast days, do not think of it as the fortress of a "jealous God" but rather as a place where all assemble, powerful and ancestral, with ceremonies giving strength.

A Taos child grows up in contact with three worlds, that of new America, old Spain and very ancient Indian. The Indian world absorbs and interprets the other two and, at fourteen that world claims him. His parents have dedicated him long ago to one of the religious societies and perhaps that society has selected him as one of those to be educated for future leadership. The religious societies are secret and the Taos in speaking English call them clans. They are not the organizations of relatives which Whites have in mind when they use that word and not like the clans of Hopi and Zuni. Whites have been asked not to inquire as to the duties of their sacred kivas, three on the north side of the village, three on the south. Each year one of them begins a long initiation, acquainting certain boys with all its ritual and preparing them for membership. Recently the white schools have come to cooperate with this system, even though it means that a boy must be absent from the classroom for eighteen months. They are preparing citizens for Taos, nor for some foreign world, so they wait without inquiry, while the boy flits in and out of the kiva and at last goes with the whole village to the sacred lake in the mountains. The girls have another sort of initiation and this, too, sets them off from the other pueblo peoples. It is seclusion for the few days when the new power of childbearing first comes on them and a little ceremony to give power for the duties for the future.

They finish school unless they want to go to a government boarding school to take a course in art or business or nursing or stockbreeding. They marry. Boys and girls who have been to a white school have learned to talk together and perhaps they have a white man's courtship, as never in the old days. Then a boy never spoke to a girl—at least publicly—until marriage. Rather he lay in wait for the maidens when they went to the river at dusk with their water jars and sought with his eyes for the smiling and plump ones, slenderness not being an asset at Taos. Of course, he must take care that the chosen one was not a relative, even a distant one, and she must be industrious or his parents would object.

One thing he had to make sure of, and must today. Let her be a Taos girl! Taos men do not go away to live with their wives like most pueblo people. Instead they bring the wives home. Taos is definite in its objection to white women, Mexicans, Navajo, even women from other pueblos. The Tewa to the south of them make magic, say the

148

Taos, and are to be feared. Hopi and Zuni allow Whites at their masked dances and so lose their power. The Keres, who are as exclusive as the Taos themselves, had still better not learn Taos secrets.

A wife from outside, if she manages to get into the pueblo at all, must be kept sedulously away from important ceremonies. Generally her husband must build himself a house outside the village wall and stay away from some ceremonies himself. If he marries a White he is simply exiled. The Taos girl is in equally hard luck if she marries a foreign man. Perhaps he lives in another pueblo and she accompanies him there, to be kept in limbo, just as Taos keeps strange wives. Perhaps they both stay at Taos criticised and suspected. Just occasionally the foreign husband is found worthy to be a Taos man and is taken into the kiva and the village life. The religious community of Taos sometimes reminds the student of the early Amish or Quakers in America and the tragedy of "marrying out of meeting".

If all goes well, both the village and the church give their blessing to the marriage: the banns are published for three days according to the old European custom brought to America long ago, and the priest marries them. They stay married, too. This puritanic community has none of the easy divorce of Hopi and Zuni. The governor, in old days, used to whip couples who did not stay together, and in this he was backed by the church since whipping was one of its punishments. The governor still reprimands the unfaithful.

He does not have to do it too frequently for his people are serious minded and busy. As in old Colonial days, a crier is constantly summoning the men for the communal duties of ditch cleaning, horse herding, even hunting in the open season. The Navajo used to call the Taos blue jays, because of this constant calling from the housetops. The man has his field of corn, beans and squash for the household, his alfalfa and wheat for sale. Probably he has cattle and if he is one of those shrewd farmers who know how to keep what they get, he may own as many as five hundred.

His cash income is the usual one for Indians and Spanish-Americans alike in this quiet corner of the world—about two hundred dollars a year. He spends it for sugar and coffee, blue jeans and calico. Perhaps over the years he selects from the overflowing goods of the White stores, a table, some chairs, some pink glass dishes and the oilcloth which is such a boon to people with little water.

All this time the young man has been as loaded with religious duties as though he served on church committees and taught a Sunday School class. The religious feasts, sometimes Catholic, sometimes pagan, punctuate the year for the Taos for they have adopted Catholicism, not as their religion, but rather as an element of their religion. Taos people dance for the deer and the buffalo and the corn; they pray in the kivas for rain; their young men run relay races to keep the sun and moon on their courses; the clowns mimic them with the strange supernatural power which allows clowns to make fun of sacred things. Besides, they hear mass in the church and celebrate the saints' days especially that of their patron, Saint Geronimo. Once a year all the adults go into the hills for their most sacred and secret ceremony, the rites at Blue Lake which they call "our church".

That lake in the course of years became surrounded with government land and was put down on the map as part of a national forest. It was visited by tourists who threw into it fish bait and picnic scraps as white visitors generally do. The Taos applied to the government about the defiling of their sacred place with unclean things. They had a claim against the United States for one hundred thousand dollars to pay for lands usurped by white settlers long ago. They would relinquish the claim, they said, if they might have the lake. The government gave them a fifty-five year lease and tourists go there no more.

Tourists visit the pueblo; they paint pictures of the sheeted figures which stalk through the plaza and down the road lined with cottonwoods to Fernando de Taos. Citizens of the pueblo could make quite an income by posing for artists if their community did not set a limit to such frivolity. To the painting of ceremonies, it opposes a decided NO. These ceremonies are "what the people live by" and their power is not to be dissipated.

Like all people exposed to the persistent impact of another culture however, they yield here and there. They have opened up a great part of the pueblo to visitors. Buses and automobiles are met by sheeted "policemen", polite as London bobbies and just as insistent on exacting obedience to the spirit as well as to the letter of the law. They see to it that the visitor's fee is paid at the Governor's house where curios are for sale; and they exact additional fees for the use of the camera. What is more, they have notions of what you ought to take with it, and every once in a while during your perambulations a soft voice comes from a wrapped sheet over your shoulder, "There's a good picture, did you take that?"

151

They would not think of calling attention to them, but there was no rule against taking the white man's *clothespins swinging against a puffy sky, beside oldtime ladders over new window frames with glass.* The clothespins are perhaps a convenience which never entered into the discussion of old versus new ways, but until very recently glazed windows were successfully resisted as a new element which might endanger the old.

The ruling power is the council. Once it was composed of the old ceremonial officers appointed for life; the cacique, the kiva chiefs, the war captain. Three hundred years ago the Spaniards installed a governor, a lieutenant governor, a fiscal, to collect church tithes; and a sacristan, to help with the service. These have grown into Taos. Even the men who have once held these Spanish offices in two or three different years belong to the council and now all the respected old men of the village attend too, but not without invitation. The crier calls out the date of the meeting and the names of all who are expected.

One cannot help noticing the likeness of this community to other religious settlements of history. All the pueblos, of course, were religious settlements but the beliefs of some are so different from those of the Whites that the likeness escapes us. Taos might in some respects be old Salem, settled by people with one belief, people who feel that their dress, their speech, even their food, are an expression of that belief and must not be changed. And like old Salem, they change though imperceptibly.

Underneath its Spanish and Indian forms, Taos is run like one of the early Puritan hamlets where it was the joy and pride of the villagers

152

to work together at their housebuilding, their harvesting, their quilting, to have the same beliefs and the same dress and to penalize anyone who deviated. Such comparison may sound strange, referring to a town which dances for its gods, even the Christian one, but Taos, like the Massachusetts Bay colony, is proud of its rigid principles and plain farming manners, a stickler for the white sheet and the moccasin even as the Pilgrims were for the drab coat and tall hat; demanding that all shall go to church (only in this case we read kiva) and that none shall marry out of meeting.

The exotic name and the flavor of Spanish romance which still hang over the town tend to obscure this basic puritanism, as does the secrecy of the inhabitants which Whites love to believe covers incredible practices, but a glance at the taciturn features of a Taos man, between his parallel braids of black hair, should warn us that here is nothing fantastic. Taos braves may dance naked, decked with cartwheels of colored feathers and uttering war whoops, but they are similar indeed to the grim settlers of Salem. They have their witches too, and their heretics, revolting to a more mystic religion. Both of them are as duly punished as they would have been in Massachusetts. In modern days Taos is as severe with the peyote religion as were the Puritans with Roger Williams. It is not for these pages to discuss the value of the peyote trance, coming from an intoxicating root which Taos young men brought in from the Plains. The elders do not care what its value is; it is not the Taos religion.

White Americans, who have long ago left behind them the small, united communities with which the United States began, look with a pang of regret at Taos and the other pueblos changing too. There is strength in this group living with common duties, common interests, common beliefs, common desires. Preachers and organizers are clamoring for this kind of cooperation but the pueblos have it. Can it be kept?

BOOKS ON THE PUEBLOS

Although it has seemed out of place to load the foregoing sketches with citations of authorities, the writer wishes to acknowledge her debt to the large number of excellent works on the pueblos, of the past and of the present, of which those most quoted are listed below.

Prehistoric Pueblos

Douglass, A. E. Dating our Prehistoric Ruins. Natural History Magazine, vol. 21, no. 1
Jenness, Diamond. The American Aborigines. University of Toronto Press, 1932.
Kidder, A. V. An Introduction to Southwestern Archaeology. Yale University Press, 1924.
Museum of Northern Arizona. Leaflets on Hopi Archaeology. Flagstaff, Ariz.

Pueblos under Spain

Hammond, George P. Don Juan de Oñate and the Founding of New Mexico. Historical Society of New Mexico, Publications in History, vol. II, 1927.
Hodge, Frederic Webb. Hawikuh, New Mexico. Southwest Museum, Los Angeles. Frederic Webb Hodge Anniversary Publication Fund, vol. 1, 1937.
Scholes, Francis V. Articles in New Mexico Historical Review.
Twitchell, Ralph Emerson. Leading Facts of New Mexican History. Cedar Rapids, Iowa. Torch Press, 1911.
Villagra, Gaspar Perez de. Historia de Nueva Mexico. Mexico, Museo Nacional.
Bandelier, Adolph and Hewitt, Edgar L. Indians of the Rio Grande Valley. University of New Mexico Press, Albuquerque, 1937.

Modern Pueblos

Beaglehole, Ernest and Pearl. Hopi of the Second Mesa. Memoirs of American Anthropological Association, no. 44.
Bunzel, Ruth. Articles on Zuni in Report of American Bureau of Ethnology, no. 47.
— The Pueblo Potter. Columbia University Press, 1929.
Dumarest, Father Noel. Notes on Cochiti, New Mexico. Memoirs of American Anthropological Association, no. 6. 1919.
Goldfrank, Esther Schiff. The Social and Ceremonial Organization of Cochiti. Ibid. no. 33. 1927.
Hewitt, Edgar L. Ancient Life in the American Southwest.
Museum of Northern Arizona. Leaflets on Hopi. Flagstaff, Ariz.
Parsons, Elsie Clews. Social Organization of the Tewa of New Mexico. Memoirs of American Anthropological Association, no. 36.
— Taos Indians. Banta Publishing Co., Menasha, Wisc. 1936.
Stevenson, Matilda Coxe. The Sia. Report of Bureau American Ethnology, no. 11. 1890.
— The Zuni Indians. Ibid. no. 23. 1904.
Voth, R. H. Publications on Hopi in Field Columbian Museum, Anthropological Series.
White, Leslie A. The Acoma Indians. Report of Bureau of American Ethnology, no. 47. 1929.
— The Pueblo of San Felipe. Memoir American Anthropological Association, no. 38.
— The Pueblo of San Domingo. Ibid. no. 43.
Reports of US War Department, Commissioner of Indian Affairs, Soil Conservation Service, Senatorial Investigation Committees.

NO LIFE FOR A LADY

by Agnes Morley Cleaveland. "Best account of frontier life from a woman's point of view yet published."—J. Frank Dobie. 6 × 9. illus. 366 pages. cloth $15.00.

DOWN THE SANTA FE TRAIL AND INTO MEXICO

The diary of Susan Shelby Magoffin 1846–1847

In June 1846 Susan Magoffin, eighteen years old and recently married, set out with her husband, a veteran Santa Fe trader, from Independence, Missouri on a trading adventure. This was the time of the American conquest of the Southwest. They first followed Kearny's Army of the West into Santa Fe. Then they followed Doniphan and his Missouri Volunteers into Chihuahua, where they stayed for months. Here we have a colorful and exciting journal of an observant young woman who travelled this region at a crucial period of American history. 6 × 9. illus. 344 pages. cloth $15.00.

MAXWELL LAND GRANT

by William A. Keleher. Here is the fascinating story of the Maxwell Land Grant, told by a man who did extensive research on the subject. The struggle for ownership and use of the Grant, which was finally declared to contain 2,680 square miles, is an interesting chapter in the history of the Southwest. 6 × 9. illus. 180 pages, plus one map. cloth $15.00.

THE RESOURCES OF NEW MEXICO—1881

prepared by the Territorial Bureau of Immigration. This is a very entertaining item of nostalgia. The elaborate typography of the ads is a true delight. The text includes a sketch of the history of New Mexico as well as a review of its resources. In the flamboyant language of the time, there is a strong plea for ambitious and enterprising men to move to New Mexico to take advantage of excellent prospects for success. 5 × 8-1/2. 76 pages. paper $1.50, cloth $9.50.

THE FLOCK

by Mary Austin. This book is a great classic of California history. It tells the story of shepherding in California beginning with the original flocks of Spanish California. Most of the book is based on Mary Austin's personal observations (circa 1900) as well as on her long conversations with the men who made shepherding their way of life. 5-1/4 × 8. illus. 276 pages. cloth $9.50.

Please order from:

William Gannon, Publisher
P.O. Box 2610
Santa Fe, New Mexico 87501

a list of other books on the Southwest:

PUEBLO INDIAN EMBROIDERY
by H. P. Mera. The Pueblo Indians of New Mexico and Arizona produced a distinctive type of embroidery which compares favorably with the folk art in needlework of Europe and elsewhere. This Southwestern native American craft is not so well known as pottery-making, weaving, and metal work, but it is important because of its uniqueness. This finely illustrated book serves as a useful introduction. 8-1/2 × 11. 23 black and white plates, 3 color plates. 80 pages. paper $7.50, cloth $16.50.

THE RAIN-MAKERS
Indians of Arizona and New Mexico.
by Mary Roberts Coolidge. "This thorough treatment of the Indians of Arizona and New Mexico contains an excellent account of the Hopi snake ceremony for bringing rain."—J. Frank Dobie. 5 × 8-1/2. illus. 366 pages. cloth $15.00.

THE CENTURIES OF SANTA FE
by Paul Horgan. The history of the city different has been recreated in an absorbing narrative by one of America's most distinguished writers. 5-1/2 × 8-1/4. illus. 380 pages. paper $6.50, cloth $15.00.

BEHIND THE MOUNTAINS
by Oliver LaFarge. These delightful stories are based on the recollections of Oliver La Farge's wife, Consuelo, of her childhood. Consuelo Baca grew up on a large ranch in the valley of Rociada in the Sangre de Cristo mountains of northern New Mexico. Here is a coloful and authentic account of the enchanting life lived by the Baca children in the 1920's. The Depression brought this life to an end when the family had to sell the ranch. This is superb writing on a way of life that has ceased to exist. 5-1/2 × 8. 192 pages. cloth $9.50.

NEW MEXICO TRIPTYCH
By Fray Angelico Chavez. This book contains three timeless stories of life in New Mexico's small, Spanish-speaking villages. 6 × 8. illus. 84 pages. paper $2.50, cloth $9.50.

ORIGINS OF NEW MEXICO FAMILIES
IN THE SPANISH COLONIAL PERIOD
by Fray Angelico Chavez. Because there were essentially two colonizations of New Mexico, the Onate conquest and the Vargas reconquest, this book is divided into two parts: the seventeenth century (1598–1693) and the eighteenth century (1693–1821). Based on years of careful research, Fray Chavez has given us not just a reference volume on the origin of particular families, but an important tool for understanding the kind of life lived by these New Mexico pioneers. 8-1/2 × 11. illus. 360 pages. paper $15.00, cloth $30.00.